THE WEALTH OF VALUES

Redefining Development through
Ethics, Family, and Society

DR. VIJAY VARADI

BRITISH NOBLE PRESS
UK • INDIA • USA

Copyright

This book is a work of non-fiction. Names and identifying details may have been changed to protect individuals' privacy. The insights, methods, and reflections presented are based on the author's personal experience in the education field and are intended to offer guidance and inspiration to educators.

Published by British Noble Press

Printed in India

*Dedicated to God, for being my constant anchor.
And to my family, for their unwavering love and support.*

Acknowledgment

This book is the outcome of a long journey of learning, unlearning, reflection, and lived experience. It would not have been possible without the contributions, support, and influence of many individuals and forces that shaped my thinking and my life.

I express my sincere gratitude to all my teachers—formal and informal—who helped me understand concepts deeply, encouraged me to question contradictions, and guided me to learn with authenticity rather than assumption. Their intellectual rigor and openness laid the foundation for critical and meaningful inquiry.

I am deeply thankful to my near and dear ones who enabled me to learn beyond theory—through real experiences and practical situations. Their lives, conversations, and challenges helped me grasp the realities behind economic principles and human behavior in ways no textbook could.

My family has been my strongest pillar of support. Their constant encouragement made it possible for me to learn, experience, understand, practice, and practically implement economic principles in everyday life. Every insight in this book is rooted in that lived support system.

I extend my heartfelt appreciation to the women whose lives and struggles revealed the invisible weight of double work—professional and personal—and its profound economic and social implications. Their resilience compelled me to revisit, rethink, and refine my perspectives on economics with greater sensitivity and responsibility.

I sincerely acknowledge the editorial team for their patience, professionalism, and meticulous commitment in reviewing, refining, and finalizing this book. Their thoughtful feedback, careful attention to detail, and unwavering support throughout the editorial process significantly strengthened the clarity, coherence, and quality of this work.

I am especially grateful to my wife, Kavitha, for her unwavering support, patience, and strength at every stage of this journey. Her belief in my work sustained me through moments of doubt and determination alike. To my daughters, Mahima and Keerthi, I owe my deepest thanks for their unconditional love, encouragement, and quiet confidence in me.

Finally, I acknowledge everyone who, directly or indirectly, contributed to shaping and cultivating who I am today—through discussions, disagreements, guidance, influence, and shared wisdom. Each interaction has left an indelible mark on this work.

Above all, I thank God, who strengthened me in every possible way—mentally, spiritually, and emotionally—to conceive, write, and complete this book.

— Dr Vijay Varadi, PhD

About the Author

Dr. Vijay Varadi is a distinguished economist, celebrated author, and a trailblazer in the field of economic development. With 18+ years of exceptional experience spanning academia and the corporate world, Dr. Vijay Varadi has left an indelible mark on the realm of economics through a profound understanding of theories, strategies, and their real-world applications.

Having earned a Ph.D. in Economics, Dr. Vijay Varadi stands as a beacon of intellectual prowess and academic excellence. With an impressive portfolio of 12 meticulously researched papers, Dr. Vijay Varadi has contributed significantly to the advancement of economic thought. These research endeavors have not only earned recognition among peers but have also sparked meaningful dialogues on pressing global economic issues.

The embodiment of knowledge and innovation, Dr. Vijay Varadi has authored four critically acclaimed books in the field of economics prior to this current endeavor. Each publication reflects a dedication to unraveling the complexities of economic systems and providing actionable insights that transcend theory. These books have earned a special place in the libraries of scholars, practitioners, and enthusiasts alike, serving as guideposts in navigating the intricate landscape of economic development.

With a unique blend of academic expertise and corporate acumen, Dr. Vijay Varadi has worn many hats, from Director of OphoTech to Professor of Golden Gate University, holding diverse roles of accountability and leadership within both spheres. This holistic perspective has bestowed a deep-rooted understanding of the symbiotic relationship between theory and practice, enriching Dr. Vijay Varadi's ability to craft strategies that resonate in the real world.

The current book, "The Wealth of Values" stands as a testament to Dr. Vijay Varadi's unparalleled grasp of the subject matter. With its culmination, Dr. Vijay Varadi not only draws upon a wealth of experience but also distills a true sense of understanding into the pages. This book is the embodiment of years of academic rigor, corporate engagement, and an unwavering commitment to driving positive change through economic growth.

As a visionary thought leader, Dr. Vijay Varadi envisions a future where economic development is not a distant dream but a tangible reality accessible to nations, regions, and communities across the globe. Through this book, Dr. Vijay Varadi invites readers to embark on a journey that marries theory with practice, fostering a world of inclusive prosperity.

Sincerely,

Dr. Vijay Varadi,

Author and Economist

Contents

Preface

In the ever-changing world of economic development, there are countless theories and strategies that aim to lead countries and societies toward sustained prosperity. However, as history has shown, achieving sustainable economic growth is a complex endeavor. In my book, "The Wealth of Values (My opinions, viewpoints, and approaches to restructuring sustainable economic development)," I delve into the multifaceted and often misunderstood realm of economic development, offering my own unique perspective.

My primary motivation for writing this book stems from a deep-seated desire to contribute to the ongoing discourse surrounding sustainable economic development. Throughout my years of study and professional experience, I have come to realize that many existing approaches often fall short of delivering long-term results. In this book, I attempt to address these shortcomings by offering new insights and alternative strategies that prioritize social responsibility, environmental conservation, and the equitable distribution of resources.

At the heart of this work lies the notion that economic development should be viewed holistically, taking into account not just economic factors but also social, environmental, and cultural elements. I advocate for a comprehensive approach that focuses on building strong communities, fostering healthy environments, and nurturing a robust, inclusive economy that benefits all members of society. By intertwining these aspects, I believe that it is possible to create a framework that truly supports sustainable development.

Drawing from a broad spectrum of sources, including scholarly research, real-world case studies, and personal observations, this book aims to provide readers with a comprehensive understanding of the challenges and opportunities associated with economic development. It is my hope that by sharing my opinions, viewpoints, and approaches, this work will serve as a valuable resource for policymakers, academics, business leaders, and anyone interested in the intricacies of sustainable economic growth.

Through these pages, one can explore various concepts and strategies that I believe hold the potential to reshape the landscape of economic development. By offering a fresh perspective, I aim to encourage a reevaluation of established practices and promote innovative thinking that prioritizes the long-term well-being of individuals, communities, and the planet as a whole.

It is my hope that this book will stimulate thoughtful discussions and inspire action toward a more equitable and sustainable future. I invite you to join me on this journey to explore the myriad ways in which we can work together to build a stronger, more resilient, and more inclusive global economy.

With gratitude and optimism,

Dr. Vijay Varadi, PhD Economics

Prologue

In corridors of economics, whispers of failure resound, As visions of sustainable growth remain unfound.

Policies short-sighted, complexity abounds, In societal fabrics, chaos unbounds.

Ecological systems teeter on the edge, As we push nature to its utmost hedge. Economical foundations crack and split, As humans live in chaos and turmoil.

Adverse effects ripple through lives so dear, In families, individuals, societies, a rising fear.

Economic and psychological transformations unfold, in stories of human struggle, untold.

Women's labor, undervalued and dismissed, Into the labor force, they're forcibly thrust. Unemployment and inflation, a growing tide,

In family structures, chaos and strife reside.

Advancements in economics, technology, and AI, bring adverse effects, and families sigh.

For well-being becomes a distant dream, As the world grapples with a new scheme.

Let us remember, as we forge ahead, the human cost, the tears we've shed. In pursuit of growth, let us not forget, The value of lives, in blood and sweat.

In a world of disparities, where power is but a dream, For many, resources scarce, unequal seems the theme. Wealth concentrated, in the hands of but a few,

As millions struggle, for a life that's just and true.

Injustice like a river, flows through society's veins,

The powerless and voiceless, bound by invisible chains. Exploitation reigns, as the strong the weak oppress,

In a world of plenty, many live with so much less.

The cries of those who suffer, rise like a mournful song, In a world of inequality, so much seems to be wrong.

With power comes corruption, like a poison in the well, The actions of the mighty, in history's pages, tell.

In this uneven landscape, conflicts often flare, Violence and strife, burdens too heavy to bear. When resources are hoarded, and power is abused, Society itself, becomes broken and confused.

The social fabric tears, as distrust starts to grow, Political upheaval, as the seeds of discontent sow.

The economy falters, as the gap between rich and poor, Widens every day, we can't ignore it anymore.

In this world of disparity, education falls behind, Healthcare out of reach, solutions hard to find. Environmental degradation, in the quest for more,

Leaves the Earth scarred, as we continue to explore.

A society divided, with injustice at its core, Cannot hope to thrive, it deserves so much more.

For the balance must be struck, between wealth and need, In a world of fairness, we all can succeed.

So let us strive for justice, in this world we share, Let us work for equity, showing that we care.

For in a world united, where resources flow to all, Society can flourish, and together, we won't fall.

Introduction

Economies have undergone significant changes and transformations over the centuries, influenced by shifts in needs and evolving ideological perspectives. These changes have introduced an array of complex and intriguing challenges for economists. Modern economic principles and theories, while evolving, have also increased the complexity of the processes involved. One of the key challenges is the disparity between real-life scenarios and the theoretical models that have been developed. Much emphasis has been placed on philosophical assumptions in the creation of economic methodologies, which often employ complex mathematical models. However, these models are limited in their ability to account for human emotions and the nuances of human interactions. Consequently, the solutions proposed by economists, while numerous, have added further complexity to the system, exacerbating the challenges faced by the contemporary economy.

This book adopts a mixed-method approach, blending data-driven economic analysis with moral and value-based reasoning to provide a holistic understanding of development.

[1] Economics fundamentally revolves around the allocation and efficient utilization of available resources to improve future outcomes. The philosophy of economics seeks to comprehend how to best satisfy human desires within the constraints of these resources. In this context, economists have dedicated their efforts to understanding and addressing the interconnections between production, supply, and distribution of goods and services, all of which rely on these resources. Over time, economic theories have evolved to tackle and formulate solutions to specific economic issues, whether they arise along a vertical or horizontal spectrum. However, these theories often address only a portion of the problem rather than providing a comprehensive solution.

[2] Addressing problems in individual sub-sectors does not necessarily lead to the comprehensive development of the entire economy. Many economic theories have neglected the need for holistic development across all sectors, instead displaying a disproportionate focus on certain sectors like services. Modern economic theories have often entirely disregarded the importance of the primary sector, particularly agriculture and its associated industries, for future generations, putting entire generations at risk. These theories have largely sidelined both agriculture and industry, despite their potential to significantly diversify the structure of economic growth and development.

Economic well-being is influenced by more than just income. It encompasses a variety of factors, including social behavior, the ability to understand and navigate various circumstances, emotional regulation in response to situations, responsible management of economic and natural resources, and adherence to public policies for the benefit of others. Unfortunately, economists have often overlooked these interconnected elements when charting a course for societal or economic development. Instead, they have fostered an illusion of progress, which has raised concerns due to the undue burden and risk placed on economies. The adoption of inappropriate economic policies, often characterized by short- sighted or partial solutions, has further exacerbated the misdirection of economic structures and policy frameworks.

[3] Economic philosophy and thought are crucial for formulating appropriate policies in consultation with political economy, taking into account political pressures. These theories should be stable and consistent over time, but unfortunately, they haven't always adhered to this principle in practice. Over the centuries, theories have often been crafted to serve either the political economy or the business community, adding confusion and chaos to the system. This is contrary to what the real situation should be, as the discrepancies between these policies and the realities on the ground become evident.

[4] The role of economists is crucial in this context. Every decision involves human judgment, and humans are not emotionless entities from another planet or unfeeling machines. Every decision carries both risks and rewards. Economists are tasked with minimizing risks and offering solutions that benefit all aspects of society. In this regard, the economy can be seen as a large family, and economists are akin to trusted physicians. Unfortunately, the solutions often prescribed by economists do not properly address the root causes of problems but instead focus on superficial issues. These prescriptions, rooted in economic philosophy and thought, are based on numerous assumptions and theories regarding human interaction and influence in decision-making processes. As a result, the systems often fail to acknowledge the true significance, necessity, and consequences of policies. To manage risks, economists have divided into specializations, prioritizing systematic changes over human emotions and assessments. This has led to a common pitfall in every field of economic theory. [5] Economic theories that ignore human decisions and interactions may not yield positive results or may even lead to harmful practices. This is a major concern as the economic challenges

faced by these systems become more complex and unique. [6]In sum, it is essential for economists to consider human emotions, interactions, and evaluations in their analyses and solutions to ensure a more holistic and effective approach to addressing economic problems.

[7] As a result, various branches of economics have been established to address specific issues within the economy. These branches have attempted to provide solutions for their respective areas, but not for the economy as a whole. Each branch of the discipline has evolved to tackle problems in the economy, offering numerous theories, strategies, and tools. However, more are still needed to fully address the complexity of the issues. This is where the motivations of economics come into play.

In this context, the motivations behind economic approaches often contribute to greater complexity in the problems rather than offering solutions for societal or human concerns.

[1] Economics is the study of how individuals, businesses, governments, and societies allocate their limited resources to satisfy their unlimited wants. It examines how decisions are made about the production, distribution, and consumption of goods and services.

- Economics is divided into two main branches:
    - **Microeconomics:** Studies the behavior of individual economic agents, such as consumers, firms, and households. It examines how these entities make decisions, how they interact in markets, and how they respond to changes in market conditions.
    - **Macroeconomics:** Examines the aggregate behavior of the entire economy. It deals with issues such as economic growth, inflation, unemployment, fiscal policy, and monetary policy.

Efficient allocation and utilization of resources are central to economic analysis. Economists study how resources are allocated among various uses and examine the trade-offs involved in these allocations. They analyze how markets coordinate these allocations and determine the price and quantity of goods and services produced.

- There are several key concepts in economics:
    - **Scarcity:** The idea that resources are limited relative to the unlimited wants and needs of individuals and societies.
    - **Opportunity Cost:** The value of the next best alternative forgone when a choice is made.
    - **Marginal Analysis:** The examination of the additional benefits and costs associated with a particular decision.
    - **Incentives:** Factors that influence and motivate people's decisions and actions.
    - **Markets:** Settings where buyers and sellers come together to exchange goods and services.

By understanding these concepts, economists can evaluate how well an economy is functioning, identify inefficiencies, and develop policies to improve outcomes for individuals and society.

[2] When attempting to solve issues within specific sub-sectors of an economy, it can sometimes have unintended consequences or fail to address the broader needs of the entire economy. This is because the economy is interconnected, and changes in one sector can have ripple effects throughout the entire economy. There are several reasons why focusing exclusively on sub-sectors may not lead to the development of all sectors:

- **Inter-dependency:** Economic sectors are often interdependent, meaning that changes in one sector can affect others.

For instance, if the government provides subsidies to the agriculture sector, it might lead to an increase in agricultural production. However, this might also result in lower prices for agricultural goods, which could hurt farmers' incomes in the long run.

- **Resource Allocation:** Solving issues in specific sub-sectors may divert resources (capital, labor, etc.) away from other sectors that also need attention. This could result in an unbalanced development where some sectors thrive while others struggle.
- **Incomplete Solutions:** Addressing problems in isolation might not lead to comprehensive solutions. For example, fixing the transportation infrastructure in one sector might not significantly benefit the economy if the energy sector is still underdeveloped.

- **Negative Spillovers:** Interventions in one sub-sector might have negative spillover effects on others. For example, if the government heavily regulates one industry, it might drive investment away from that industry and into others, leading to an imbalance in economic development.
- **External Factors:** Many factors that affect economic development, such as global trade, technological advancements, and geopolitical events, are not confined to a single sub-sector. Addressing issues in individual sub-sectors might not account for these broader influences.
- **Short-term vs. Long-term Perspective:** Solving issues in sub-sectors might be beneficial in the short term but might not align with the long-term needs of the entire economy. It's crucial to consider both immediate and future impacts when addressing economic issues.
- **Political Considerations:** Sometimes, decisions to address issues in specific sub-sectors might be driven by political considerations rather than a comprehensive analysis of what's best for the entire economy. This can lead to policies that prioritize certain sectors at the expense of others.

[3] Indeed, economic philosophy and thought are essential components of policy-making, as they provide the theoretical framework within which policies are formulated. When combined with insights from political economy, these tools can help policymakers navigate complex issues and political pressures to develop more effective policies.

Here's how economic philosophy and thought, combined with political economy, contribute to policy-making:

- **Understanding the Role of Markets:** Different economic philosophies have different views on the role of markets in allocating resources and promoting economic development. For example, classical economists advocate for minimal government intervention in the markets, while Keynesian's believe that government intervention is necessary to stabilize the economy. Understanding these different perspectives helps policymakers strike a balance between market forces and government intervention.
- **Setting Policy Objectives:** Economic theories provide a framework for setting policy objectives. For instance, monetarists focus on controlling inflation through monetary policy, while supply-side economists emphasize the importance of encouraging production and investment. By understanding these different perspectives, policymakers can set priorities and objectives that align with their economic goals.
- **Analyzing Trade-offs:** Economic thought helps policymakers understand the trade-offs involved in different policy choices. For example, expansionary fiscal policy might boost economic growth in the short term but could lead to higher inflation or fiscal deficits in the long run. Economic theories help policymakers weigh the pros and cons of different policy options.
- **Navigating Political Pressures:** Political economy examines how political and economic factors interact and influence each other. It helps policymakers understand how political pressures, power dynamics, and institutional structures impact economic outcomes. This knowledge is crucial for formulating policies that are politically feasible and can achieve desired economic outcomes.

- **Incorporating Historical Lessons:** Economic thought has evolved over time based on historical experiences and empirical evidence. By studying the history of economic thought, policymakers can learn from past successes and failures and avoid repeating mistakes.

- **Encouraging Debates and Critiques:** Economic philosophy and thought encompass a wide range of perspectives and approaches. Encouraging debates and critiques of different economic theories helps policymakers evaluate different viewpoints and develop more robust and well-rounded policies.

- Adapting to Changing Contexts: Economic conditions and political dynamics change over time. By Understanding the principles of economics thought and political economy, policymakers can adapt their approaches to suit changing circumstances and achieve desired outcomes.

In conclusion, economic philosophy and thought, combined with insights from political economy, provide policymakers with valuable tools to navigate complex issues, understand trade-offs, and formulate policies that are both economically sound and politically feasible.

[4] It is true that sometimes economic policies may not address the root causes of problems and instead focus on superficial or symptomatic issues. This can happen for several reasons:

- **Complexity of Economic Systems:** Economies are complex, interconnected systems, and the root causes of problems can be difficult to identify. Policies may focus on easily observable symptoms rather than the underlying factors contributing to those symptoms. For instance, a policy might aim to reduce unemployment by creating temporary government jobs but may not address the deeper issues, such as skill mismatches, structural changes in the economy, or barriers to private sector job creation.
- **Political Pressures:** Policymakers often face political pressures to deliver quick results, especially during election cycles. As a result, they may be incentive to implement policies that provide immediate relief but do not address deeper issues. These "band-aid" solutions can be popular with voters in the short term but may not provide long-term benefits.
- **Lack of Data or Information:** Policymakers may not have access to the data or information needed to diagnose the root causes of problems accurately. For instance, data on informal economic activities or the experiences of marginalized groups may be scarce, making it difficult to design policies that address the needs of these populations.
- **Cognitive Biases:** Policymakers, like all individuals, are susceptible to cognitive biases. They may be influenced by prevailing economic orthodoxies, personal beliefs, or ideological convictions. This can lead to policies that focus on certain aspects of a problem while ignoring others.
- **Institutional Constraints:** Policymakers may face institutional constraints that limit their ability to address root causes. For example, a central bank may have a mandate to control inflation but may not have the tools or authority to address the structural issues driving inflation.

- **Short-Term vs. Long-Term Trade-offs:** Some policies may provide short-term benefits at the expense of long-term outcomes. Policymakers may prioritize immediate gains over long-term solutions, especially if the benefits of addressing root causes are not immediately apparent.
- **Incomplete Theories:** Economic theories are often based on simplified models that make assumptions about human behavior, market dynamics, and other factors. In practice, the real-world economy is much more complex, and policies based on these models may not fully address the root causes of problems.
- **Unintended Consequences:** Economic policies can have unintended consequences, and solutions that seem effective at addressing one issue may inadvertently exacerbate other problems. Policymakers may struggle to anticipate and manage these complex interactions.

To address root causes effectively, policymakers should take a holistic approach, considering multiple factors and their interconnections. They should also be open to revising policies based on new evidence and changing circumstances. Collaboration with experts from various fields, including sociology, political science, and environmental science, can provide valuable insights into the root causes of economic problems and help design more effective policies.

[5] Economics is fundamentally about human behavior—how people make choices and interact with each other in the context of scarcity. Ignoring the human element in economic theories can lead to flawed models and policies that fail to deliver positive results or even cause harm. This pitfall can manifest in several ways:

- **Rationality Assumption:** Traditional economic models often assume that individuals are perfectly rational, meaning they always make decisions that maximize their self-interest. However, behavioral economics has shown that people often act irrationally, influenced by emotions, biases, and social factors. Ignoring these behavioral elements can lead to policies that are ineffective or even counterproductive.

- **Homogeneity Assumption:** Economic models sometimes assume that all individuals are alike and respond similarly to changes in prices, incentives, and other factors. In reality, people have diverse preferences, needs, and constraints. Policies based on such assumptions may fail to address the unique needs of different groups and may exacerbate inequalities.

- **Exclusion of Social and Cultural Factors:** Economic models often focus on monetary incentives and market mechanisms, overlooking the influence of social norms, cultural values, and social interactions on economic behavior. Ignoring these factors can result in policies that are culturally insensitive or fail to account for social dynamics.

- **Short-Term Focus:** Economic models and policies may prioritize short-term outcomes, such as boosting GDP growth or reducing inflation, without considering long-term consequences, including environmental sustainability, social cohesion, and well-being. This short-term focus can lead to harmful practices that undermine long-term goals.

- **Over-reliance on Quantitative Metrics:** Economic models often rely heavily on quantitative metrics, such as GDP, inflation, and unemployment rates, to evaluate policy outcomes. These metrics may not capture all aspects of human well-being, including health, happiness, and social connections. Policies based solely on these metrics may fail to address broader societal goals.
- **Incomplete Understanding of Interactions:** Economic models may not fully account for the complex interactions between individuals, firms, and institutions, leading to policies that do not consider the ripple effects of interventions. For example, imposing tariffs on imports may protect domestic industries in short term but may lead to trade wars and negative consequences for consumers and other sectors in the long run.

To avoid these pitfalls, economic theories and policies should incorporate insights from behavioral economics, sociology, anthropology, and other fields. They should consider the diversity of human preferences and needs, the influence of social and cultural factors, and the long-term consequences of policy choices. By taking a more holistic and human-centered approach, economists can develop more effective and inclusive policies that enhance overall well-being.

- **Short-Term Focus:** Economic models and policies may prioritize short-term outcomes, such as boosting GDP growth or reducing inflation, without considering long-term consequences, including environmental sustainability, social cohesion, and well-being. This short-term focus can lead to harmful practices that undermine long-term goals.

- **Over-reliance on Quantitative Metrics:** Economic models often rely heavily on quantitative metrics, such as GDP, inflation, and unemployment rates, to evaluate policy outcomes. These metrics may not capture all aspects of human well-being, including health, happiness, and social connections. Policies based solely on these metrics may fail to address broader societal goals.
- **Incomplete Understanding of Interactions:** Economic models may not fully account for the complex interactions between individuals, firms, and institutions, leading to policies that do not consider the ripple effects of interventions. For example, imposing tariffs on imports may protect domestic industries in the short term but may lead to trade wars and negative consequences for consumers and other sectors in the long run.

To avoid these pitfalls, economic theories and policies should incorporate insights from behavioral economics, sociology, anthropology, and other fields. They should consider the diversity of human preferences and needs, the influence of social and cultural factors, and the long-term consequences of policy choices. By taking a more holistic and human-centered approach, economists can develop more effective and inclusive policies that enhance overall well-being.

[6] economic models and theories may overly focus on concepts like scarcity and resource allocation, leading to under-emphasis on the role of human behavior. While scarcity is indeed a fundamental concept in economics, an exclusive focus on it can result in a narrow and incomplete view of economic phenomena. This can lead to the creation of models that are too simplistic or not representative of real-world behavior.

The shift towards recognizing the importance of human behavior in economic analysis has been fueled by the development of behavioral economics, which integrates insights from psychology into economic models.

Behavioral economics challenges the traditional assumption of perfect rationality and incorporates factors such as emotions, biases, and social influences into economic analysis. Some key contributions of behavioral economics include:

- Bounded Rationality: People often have limited information, cognitive capacity, and time to make decisions. As a result, they may use shortcuts or heuristics to make choices, which may not always be perfectly rational.

- **Loss Aversion:** People tend to feel the pain of losses more intensely than the pleasure of equivalent gains. This can affect decision-making, especially in contexts involving risk and uncertainty.
- **Present Bias:** People often give more weight to immediate gratification than to future benefits. This can result in behaviors such as procrastination or insufficient saving for retirement.
- **Social Preferences:** People's decisions are often influenced by social norms, peer pressure, and a desire for fairness or altruism. These factors can shape behavior in ways that deviate from purely self-interested behavior.
- **Framing Effects:** The way information is presented can influence people's choices. For example, people may respond differently to a tax presented as a "penalty" versus a "bonus."

Behavioral economics has enriched economic analysis by providing a more nuanced and realistic understanding of human behavior. It has also led to the design of policies that are more effective in achieving desired outcomes. For example, "nudges" are interventions that leverage behavioral insights to encourage better choices without restricting options. These have been used in areas such as promoting healthier eating, increasing retirement savings, and reducing energy consumption.

In conclusion, while scarcity remains a central concept in economics, it is essential to recognize the role of human behavior in shaping economic outcomes. Incorporating insights from behavioral economics and other disciplines can lead to a more comprehensive and realistic understanding of economic phenomena and the design of more effective policies.

[7] the recognition of the limitations and complexities of human behavior in the context of economics has led to the development of specialized branches of economics. These branches attempt to address specific issues within the economy and offer a more detailed analysis of particular economic phenomena. Some of these branches include:

- **Behavioral Economics:** Focuses on understanding how psychological factors, such as emotions and cognitive biases, influence economic decision-making. Behavioral economics challenges the traditional assumption of perfect rationality and explores the impact of irrational behavior on economic outcomes.
- **Microeconomics:** Studies individual economic agents, such as consumers and firms, and their interactions in markets. Microeconomics examines how individuals make choices regarding consumption, production, and resource allocation.

- **Macroeconomics:** Analyzes the economy as a whole, including aggregate indicators such as GDP, inflation, and unemployment. Macroeconomics explores the factors that drive economic growth, business cycles, and long-term trends.
- **Development Economics:** Investigates the economic challenges and opportunities faced by developing countries. Development economics explores topics such as poverty, inequality, and economic growth.
- **Environmental Economics:** Examines the interaction between the economy and the environment. Environmental economics focuses on issues such as pollution, natural resource management, and climate change.
- **Health Economics:** Studies the economics of healthcare and health-related behaviors. Health economics explores topics such as healthcare financing, health insurance, and the impact of health on economic outcomes.
- **Labor Economics:** Analyzes the dynamics of the labor market, including employment, wages, and productivity. Labor economics investigates factors that affect labor supply and demand, such as education, skills, and labor market regulations.
- **Public Economics:** Explores the role of government in the economy, including taxation, public spending, and regulation. Public economics examines the impact of government policies on economic outcomes and the design of optimal policies.
- **International Economics:** Studies economic interactions between countries, including trade, investment, and exchange rates. International economics explores the benefits and challenges of globalization and international economic cooperation.

- **Industrial Organization:** Investigates the structure and behavior of firms and industries. Industrial organization explores topics such as competition, market power, and regulation.

Each of these branches of economics provides valuable insights into specific economic issues and offers tools to address the challenges facing the economy. By combining the expertise of various branches, policymakers and economists can develop more comprehensive and effective solutions to economic problems.

CHAPTER 1

What Development Really Means

Throughout history, economists from Adam Smith to recent Nobel laureates have drawn from disciplines such as mathematics, statistics, game theory, and optimization to address complex questions of economic development[8]. Their recommendations, grounded in rigorous analysis, have often advocated for deep investigation into the root causes of economic challenges faced by nations. However, a significant critique emerges: most economic thought has tended to overlook the pivotal role of society in shaping development outcomes. As a result, many policy recommendations have fallen short, sometimes exacerbating existing problems rather than solving them. The persistence of these "leaking holes" continues to hinder the sustainable growth and development of economies[9].

While certain economic policies have scored successes, there must be a sober evaluation of whether these policies genuinely elevate human standards, both societal and individual. Economists are increasingly called upon to address this gap by prioritizing solutions that not only yield wealth but also advance well-being, justice, and resilience across societies[10].

A prevailing limitation in modern economic analysis is the tendency to focus narrowly on monetary measures, wealth, income, and financial flows while under-emphasizing critical factors such as social context, education, health, law, politics, religion, and broader societal structures. This wealth-centric lens has led to intensified imbalances in economic equilibrium, heightened complexity in economic systems, anomalous business cycles, and unforeseen macroeconomic uncertainties. By overlooking these broader determinants, contemporary economic policy risks producing results that are not only incomplete but, at times, destabilizing.

A singular focus on financial indicators like GDP growth, inflation, or employment fails to capture the full spectrum of forces contributing to overall well-being, economic durability, and long-term growth. Here are some of the ways excessive emphasis on wealth alone can negatively impact economies:

1. **Economic Equilibrium Imbalances:** Prioritizing material gain can lead to income inequalities and gaps in essential services such as education and healthcare, creating social tension and stifling long-run growth.

2. **Increased Economic Complexity:** Disregarding social and cultural context makes economies harder to predict and manage, increasing systemic volatility and uncertainty.

3. **Abnormal Business Cycles:** Overemphasis on wealth accumulation is linked to speculative bubbles and financial instability, resulting in extreme boom-bust cycles.

4. **Macroeconomic Imbalances:** Such policies may cause chronic trade deficits, unsustainable debt, and asset bubbles, threatening economic stability.

5. **Unprecedented Uncertainties:** Ignoring non-monetary factors makes economies vulnerable to shocks that are difficult to foresee using traditional monetary metrics alone. To move toward sustainable and equitable economic development, analysis and policy must embrace a multidimensional view, one that integrates social, educational, legal, political, and cultural factors alongside economic ones. This holistic approach is essential for enhancing human flourishing, resilience, and inclusivity.

6. **Positive and Normative Economics:** Complementary Perspectives

7. **Economics is conventionally divided into two distinct but interconnected branches:** Positive Economics is factual and descriptive, analyzing what is how economies function and how different variables interact using empirical evidence that can be tested and validated.

Normative Economics addresses what ought to be, embedding judgments, ethics, and social goals into policy prescriptions. It asks whether proposed policies align with broader societal aims and principles, making recommendations that reflect prevailing values and

This distinction is critical; while positive economics provides the data and models for understanding effects, normative economics guides the ethical evaluation and selection of policies. In practice, policymakers rely on both empirical insights to inform and value-driven frameworks to decide.

Increasingly, it is recognized that an over-reliance on positive, descriptive analysis while neglecting normative values and public policy can produce a short-sighted focus on individual gain rather than collective welfare. This is evident in economic models based on rational self-interest, a core tenet of classical and neoclassical thought originating with Smith. While useful for some predictions, such models have clear limitations; they risk overlooking equity, ethics, and collective goods vital for balanced development.

Historical approaches, centered on personal gain or rational self-interest, have sometimes treated public policy as an extension of individual ambition, ignoring societal needs. This approach is problematic for several reasons:

1. **Correcting Market Failures:** Public policy is needed to address inefficiencies in markets, whether from externalities or information gaps.

2. **Ensuring Equity:** Distributional effects and justice must be weighed alongside efficiency to guarantee broadly shared prosperity.

3. **Reflecting Social Preferences:** Individuals and societies prioritize more than self-interest–altruism, community, and fairness all shape economic decisions.

4. **Providing Public Goods:** Essential goods and services generally require coordinated policy intervention to be accessible for all.

5. **Safeguarding the Future:** Ethical considerations about inter-generational equity and sustainability are essential for long-term planning.

6. **Fostering Democratic Engagement:** Transparent consideration of values and policy trade-offs promotes legitimacy and public trust.

Economics is traditionally divided into two main branches: positive economics and normative economics. These two branches approach economic questions from different perspectives and serve different purposes.

1. **Positive Economics:** This branch of economics deals with facts and objective observations. It focuses on describing and analyzing economic phenomena as they are, without making judgments or prescribing solutions. Positive economics aims to understand how the economy works and what the relationships are between different economic variables. It seeks to answer questions such as "What happens when the government increases taxes?" or "What is the impact of a minimum wage increase on employment?" The findings in positive economics are typically based on empirical evidence and can be tested and validated through observation and experimentation.

2. This branch of economics deals with opinions, judgments, and prescriptions. It focuses on what ought to be rather than what is. Normative economics involves making value judgments and recommendations based on ethical principles, societal goals, or individual preferences. It seeks to answer questions such as "Should the government increase taxes?" or "Is it fair to have a minimum wage?" The conclusions in normative economics are subjective and depend on the values and beliefs of the person making the judgments.

It's essential to distinguish between these two branches of economics because they serve different purposes and have different implications for policy making. Positive economics provides the data, models, and analysis needed to understand the effects of various economic policies, while normative economics provides a framework for evaluating and choosing between different policy options based on ethical considerations and societal goals.

Policymakers often use the insights from positive economics to inform their decisions, but the final policy choices are ultimately influenced by normative considerations.

In conclusion, true economic development is not achieved solely through wealth maximization or individual advantage. It demands that economists and policymakers balance private aspirations with the broader public good, using rigorous analysis in tandem with ethical reflection. Only by considering the full spectrum of social, cultural, political, and economic forces can societies construct robust, inclusive, and sustainable development.

[8] Creating a comprehensive list of all Nobel Prize winners in economics, along with their contributions, would be quite extensive. However, I can provide you with an overview of some notable winners, including Adam Smith, who is considered the "father of economics," though he didn't win a Nobel Prize as the award wasn't established until 1968. Here are some highlights:

> **Adam Smith** (1723-1790) - Although not a Nobel Prize winner, his work laid the foundation for modern economics. In "The Wealth of Nations" (1776), he introduced the concept of the invisible hand and advocated for free-market capitalism.

Paul Samuelson (1915-2009, Nobel Prize 1970) - Contributed to the development of modern microeconomics and macroeconomics. He wrote the influential textbook "Economics," which has been translated into numerous languages.

Milton Friedman (1912-2006, Nobel Prize 1976) - A leading figure in monetarism, he argued that inflation is primarily caused by an excessive supply of money and advocated for limited government intervention in the economy.

John Nash (1928-2015, Nobel Prize 1994) - Made fundamental contributions to game theory, particularly the concept of Nash equilibrium, which describes the outcome of a game in which each player's strategy is optimal given the strategies of other players.

Amartya Sen (b. 1933, Nobel Prize 1998) - Known for his work on welfare economics, social choice theory, and development economics. He has contributed to the understanding of poverty, inequality, and human development.

Joseph Stiglitz (b. 1943, Nobel Prize 2001) - Made contributions to the theory of asymmetric information, which explores how markets function when one party has more information than the other. He has also written extensively on inequality and globalization.

Daniel Kahneman (b. 1934, Nobel Prize 2002) - A psychologist who won the Nobel Prize in economics for his work on behavioral economics, particularly the development of prospect theory, which explains how people make decisions under uncertainty.

Paul Krugman (b. 1953, Nobel Prize 2008) - Known for his work on international trade and economic geography. He developed the "new trade theory" and "new economic geography," which explain the patterns of trade and the location of economic activity.

Esther Duflo (b. 1972, Nobel Prize 2019) - Recognized for her work on poverty alleviation and development economics. She has conducted numerous randomized controlled trials to evaluate the impact of various interventions on poverty.

Paul R. Milgrom (b. 1948, Nobel Prize 2020) and Robert B. Wilson (b. 1937, Nobel Prize 2020) - Awarded the Nobel Prize for their work on auction theory and the design of innovative auction formats.

These economists have made significant contributions to the field of economics, providing valuable insights into various economic phenomena and helping to shape economic policy. Their work continues to influence contemporary economic thought and policy making.

[9] The metaphor of a "leaking hole" suggests that despite efforts to repair or improve the economic system, persistent underlying issues continue to drain resources, potential, or growth. If the root causes of economic problems are not adequately addressed, any solutions implemented may only offer temporary relief, similar to patching up a hole that keeps leaking. Here's how such superficial or misdirected approaches can exacerbate existing economic issues:

- **Short-Term Fixes vs. Long-Term Solutions:** Implementing policies aimed at quick fixes can lead to long- term problems. For example, excessive borrowing might temporarily boost economic growth, but over the long term, it can lead to unsustainable debt levels and financial crises.
- **Misallocation of Resources:** If policies do not align with the actual needs or potential growth areas of the economy, resources (capital, labor, technology) might be wasted on unproductive sectors.
- **Exacerbating Inequalities:** Policies that do not consider the distributional impacts can exacerbate wealth and income inequalities, leading to social unrest and reduced economic mobility.
- **Creating Dependence:** Over-reliance on short-term stimulus or subsidies can create dependency and stifle innovation and competitiveness in the long run.
- **Unintended Consequences:** Without a deep understanding of the underlying issues, policies might lead to unintended negative consequences. For example, price controls intended to make goods more affordable can lead to shortages if they are set below equilibrium levels.
- **Regulatory Capture:** If regulatory bodies are overly influenced by the industries they regulate, policies may disproportionately favor specific interest groups at the expense of the general public.
- **Ignoring Externalities:** Failing to account for external costs (like pollution) in economic policies can lead to environmental degradation and long-term economic costs.
- **Lack of Adaptability:** Policies that do not account for changing global dynamics, technological advancements, or demographic shifts may quickly become obsolete or counterproductive.

- **Eroding Trust:** Repeatedly applying ineffective solutions can erode public trust in institutions, making it harder to implement necessary reforms in the future.

To avoid the "leaking hole" scenario, it's essential for policymakers to take a comprehensive, well-researched, and long-term approach to economic problems. This might involve collaborating with experts across various fields, considering the experiences of other nations, and regularly reviewing and adapting policies based on feedback and changing circumstances.

[10] Highlighting a significant critique of contemporary economic analysis and policy making, which often focuses primarily on monetary and financial indicators such as GDP growth, inflation, and employment levels. While these metrics are essential for understanding the economy's overall health, they do not capture the full range of factors that contribute to societal well-being, economic stability, and sustainable growth.

Here's how an excessive focus on wealth or money, to the detriment of other key factors, can have negative consequences:

- **Economic Equilibrium Imbalances:** By prioritizing monetary gains over other dimensions of well-being, societies might experience imbalances, such as income inequality or disparities in access to essential services like education and healthcare. These imbalances can create social unrest and hinder long-term economic growth.
- **Increased Economic Complexity:** Ignoring the social context and other non-monetary factors can lead to overly complex economic systems that are hard to understand, predict, and manage. This complexity can create volatility and uncertainty, making it challenging for policymakers and businesses to plan for the future.

- **Unusual Business Cycles:** Overemphasis on wealth accumulation might lead to speculative bubbles, financialization of the economy, and unusual business cycle fluctuations. These factors can exacerbate boom-bust cycles, create financial instability, and ultimately harm long-term economic prospects.
- **Macroeconomic Imbalances:** Excessive focus on monetary indicators can result in macroeconomic imbalances such as trade deficits, unsustainable debt levels, and asset bubbles. These imbalances can pose significant risks to financial stability and economic growth.
- **Unprecedented Uncertainties:** Overlooking non-monetary factors like political, social, and cultural contexts can lead to unanticipated shocks and crises that are hard to predict and manage. These uncertainties can create volatile economic conditions and hinder long-term planning and investment.

Incorporating a more holistic view of economics, which considers factors such as social context, education, health, law, politics, religion, and societal structures, is crucial for achieving sustainable and equitable economic development. By taking a broader perspective that considers these factors, policymakers can better understand the underlying drivers of economic behavior, design policies that promote long-term well-being, and address imbalances that could otherwise undermine economic stability and growth.

It is essential for economic analysis and policy making to incorporate a multidimensional view of well-being that goes beyond monetary metrics. By considering a broad range of factors that contribute to human flourishing, societies can build more resilient, sustainable, and inclusive economies.

CHAPTER 2

Institutions, Behavior, and Acceptance

Understanding Society's Philosophy and Structure

Economists need to grasp the philosophy and structure of society in order to provide solutions to complex economic problems. Absolutely, economists must understand the philosophy and structure of society to address complex economic problems effectively. Here's why this is crucial:

1. **Context Matters:** Economic problems do not occur in isolation. They are embedded within the social, cultural, and political fabric of a society. Understanding these contexts allows economists to offer more relevant and effective solutions.

2. **Institutional Framework:** The institutions of a society, including its legal system, governance structures, and cultural norms, influence economic behavior and

outcomes. Recognizing the role of institutions helps economists design policies that are compatible with the existing institutional framework or advocate for institutional reforms if necessary.

3. **Interdisciplinary Insights:** Complex economic problems often have roots in other disciplines such as sociology, psychology, or political science. Drawing insights from these fields can provide a richer and more comprehensive understanding of the issues at hand.

4. **Addressing Inequality:** Economic policies can have differential impacts on various segments of society. Understanding the structure of society, including its class, racial, and gender divisions, allows economists to design policies that promote equity and inclusiveness.

5. **Behavioral Insights:** People's economic behavior is influenced by social norms, beliefs, and values. Incorporating insights from philosophy and social sciences can help economists understand human behavior better and design policies that align with people's motivations and preferences.

6. **Public Acceptance:** For economic policies to be successful, they need to be accepted and supported by the public. Understanding the philosophy and values of a society can help economists design policies that resonate with people's beliefs and garner public support.

7. **Sustainable Solutions:** Addressing complex economic problems requires long-term, sustainable solutions. Understanding the philosophy and structure of society can help economists design policies that are sustainable

and compatible with the long-term goals and values of society.

In conclusion, a holistic and multidisciplinary approach that considers the philosophy and structure of society is essential for addressing complex economic problems effectively. Economists need to look beyond traditional economic models and incorporate insights from other fields and disciplines to design comprehensive and sustainable solutions.

Economic development is commonly understood as the progression of a country's or region's economic growth for the benefit of its residents. In policy making, economic development can be characterized as initiatives aimed at enhancing economic prosperity and quality of life in a community through the creation or retention of jobs, as well as the support or expansion of income and the tax base.

Governmental strategies targeting overarching economic goals like price stability, higher employment, and sustained growth. These encompass monetary and fiscal measures, financial institution regulations, and trade and taxation guidelines. Initiatives and programs that supply essential infrastructure and services, ranging from highways and parks to affordable housing, crime prevention, and primary to secondary education.

Specific measures aimed directly at creating and retaining jobs, which include efforts in business financing, marketing, community development, support for small businesses, business continuity and expansion, technological integration, and property development.

Professor Dudley Seers defines development as being about outcomes, stating that development happens when there is a reduction or elimination of poverty, inequality, and unemployment within a growing economy. According to Professor M. Todaro, development entails producing more essential goods, such as food, shelter, and healthcare, and ensuring their wider distribution. It also involves raising living standards and individual self-esteem while expanding economic and social choices and reducing fear.

Indeed, the goal of addressing complex economic problems extends beyond mere economic indicators and financial metrics. The ultimate aim is to improve the well-being of individuals and communities, providing them with more choices and opportunities, enhancing their self-esteem, and reducing fears associated with poverty, unemployment, or social inequality.

Here are some ways in which addressing economic problems holistically can contribute to these broader goals:

1. **Raising Living Standards:** Economic policies that promote growth, create jobs, and reduce inequality can raise living standards, providing individuals with greater access to essential goods and services, better housing, and improved quality of life.

2. **Enhancing Self-Esteem:** Economic empowerment can boost self-esteem, as economically secure individuals are more likely to have a positive self-image, increased confidence, and a sense of autonomy.

3. **Expanding Choices:** Economic growth and development can provide individuals with more choices and opportunities, allowing them to pursue their interests, fulfill their potential, and enjoy a wider range of experiences.

4. **Reducing Fear:** Economic security minimizes the fear

and stress associated with unemployment, poverty, or financial instability. This can improve mental health, strengthen social ties, and foster a sense of belonging and community.

5. **Promoting Social Inclusion:** Addressing economic inequality and discrimination can foster social inclusion, ensuring that all individuals, regardless of their background, have access to opportunities and can participate fully in society.

6. **Ensuring Sustainability:** Economic policies that prioritize environmental sustainability can reduce the fear of future environmental degradation, providing individuals and communities with a sense of security about their long-term well-being.

7. **Building Resilience:** Economic policies that enhance resilience to shocks, such as natural disasters or economic crises, can reduce fear and provide individuals with a sense of stability and confidence in their ability to cope with challenges.

Ultimately, addressing complex economic problems requires a multidimensional approach that considers not only financial and economic indicators but also broader aspects of human well-being. This includes raising living standards, enhancing self-esteem, expanding choices, and reducing fear. By pursuing these broader goals, economists and policymakers can contribute to creating societies that are more equitable, inclusive, and resilient.

Based on the definitions mentioned earlier, several key elements contribute to economic growth and development. These include well-being, quality of life (which encompasses food, shelter, and healthcare), efforts to support or expand incomes and the tax base, price stability, sustainable growth, crime prevention, and the reduction or elimination of poverty, income inequality, and unemployment. Additionally, development involves expanding economic and social choices while reducing fear. On the other hand, economic growth is specifically defined as an increase in a particular metric, such as real national income or GDP.

Economic growth is typically defined as the increase in the value of goods and services produced by an economy over time. It is often measured by the rate of change in Gross Domestic Product (GDP), which is the total value of all goods and services produced within a country's borders in a specific time period. Economic growth can also be measured using other indicators such as Gross National Product (GNP), which includes income earned by a country's residents both domestically and internationally.

There are two main types of economic growth:

1. Nominal Growth: This is the growth of an economy without adjusting for inflation. It includes the increase in production due to both higher prices and increased output.

2. Real Growth: This is the growth of an economy after adjusting for inflation. It only accounts for the increase in production due to increased output.

Economic growth is an essential goal for many economies, as it can lead to several positive outcomes:

1. Higher Incomes: Economic growth leads to increased incomes for individuals, which can improve their living standards and well-being.

2. Job Creation: Economic growth is associated with increased demand for goods and services, which leads to more job opportunities and lower unemployment rates.

3. Government Revenue: Economic growth boosts tax revenue for the government, which can then be used for public investments in infrastructure, education, health, and other essential services.

4. Improved Public Services: With more resources, the government can improve public services such as healthcare, education, and social welfare programs.

5. Innovation and Technological Advancements: Economic growth often comes with increased investments in research and development, leading to innovation and technological advancements.

However, it is essential to note that economic growth is not the only metric for assessing an economy's health and well-being. Other factors such as income distribution, environmental sustainability, and social inclusion are crucial for achieving holistic development. Additionally, excessive focus on economic growth without considering its broader social and environmental impacts can lead to inequality, environmental degradation, and other long-term negative consequences.

Economic Growth refers to the rise in the value of goods and services produced by an economy. It is typically measured as the percentage rate of increase in real GDP, where "real" indicates that the measurement is adjusted for inflation to remove its impact on the price of the goods and services produced. In economic terms, "economic growth" usually refers to the growth of "potential output," which is the production level at "full employment" resulting from an increase in aggregate demand or actual output. The field of Economic Growth and Development economics primarily focuses on identifying the factors that drive economic growth.

The field of Economic Growth and Development Economics studies the processes that promote the growth and development of an economy. These two areas of economics, although closely related, focus on different aspects of economic progress.

1. Economic Growth: This area is primarily concerned with increasing the output of an economy over time, as measured by metrics like GDP or GNP. Economists in this field study factors that drive growth, such as capital accumulation, technological progress, and labor force expansion.

2. Development Economics: This field focuses on improving living standards, reducing poverty, and promoting sustainable development in low-income countries. Development economists study factors like education, health, infrastructure, and institutional development.

Here are some key factors that both fields examine:

- Physical Capital: Investment in machinery, equipment, and infrastructure can boost productivity and promote economic growth.

- Human Capital: Investments in education and health improve the skills, knowledge, and well-being of the workforce, contributing to economic development.

- Technological Progress: Innovations and advancements in technology can increase efficiency, reduce costs, and drive economic growth.

- Institutions and Governance: Effective institutions, good governance, and the rule of law are crucial for economic development, as they create an environment conducive to investment and growth.

- Trade and Globalization: Openness to trade and integration into the global economy can promote growth by providing access to larger markets, technology transfer, and foreign direct investment.

- Natural Resources: Proper management of natural resources can provide a source of income, contribute to economic growth, and support sustainable development.

- Sociocultural Factors: Cultural values, social norms, and societal structures can influence economic behavior and development outcomes.

- Environmental Sustainability: Sustainable management of natural resources and environmental conservation are essential for long-term economic development.

- Income Distribution: Equitable distribution of income and wealth is crucial for social stability and inclusive development.

Both Economic Growth and Development Economics aim to understand how economies can grow and develop in a sustainable and inclusive manner. While economic growth is necessary for development, it is not sufficient on its own. Development economics focuses on broader aspects of well-being, including poverty reduction, education, health, and social inclusion, to achieve holistic and sustainable development.

The Role of Key Factors in Growth

The growth in output per capita of a country over an extended period is often explained by several factors, which are also used to account for differences in output per capita between countries. These commonly studied factors include the rate of investment, population growth, and technological change. From this, we can identify the following key factors that influence economic growth: potential output, full employment, output per capita, rate of investment, population growth, and technological change.

To achieve potential per capita output, many economists have proposed various economic strategies. However, these strategies are currently posing challenges to both economists and the economy, as they have inadvertently introduced more societal problems. This is because they were based on the assumption that the growth and development of the economy is solely about attaining potential per capita output.

Economists have proposed a wide range of strategies to increase per capita output and promote economic growth and development. Here are some of the most commonly cited strategies:

- **Investment in Physical Capital:** Increasing investments in infrastructure, machinery, and equipment can boost productivity and per capita output.

- **Investment in Human Capital:** Promoting education, training, and healthcare can improve the skills and well-being of the workforce, leading to increased productivity and per capita output.

- **Technological Progress and Innovation:** Encouraging research and development, technological progress, and innovation can increase efficiency, reduce costs, and drive economic growth.

- **Trade and Openness:** Engaging in international trade and opening up to the global economy can provide access to larger markets, technology transfer, and foreign direct investment, promoting economic growth.

- **Macroeconomic Stability:** Maintaining stable inflation, interest rates, and exchange rates can create a conducive environment for investment and growth.

- **Institutional Development:** Building strong and effective institutions, ensuring good governance, and upholding the rule of law can create a favorable environment for economic growth.

- **Market-Oriented Reforms:** Implementing market-oriented reforms, reducing bureaucratic red tape, and promoting competition can boost economic efficiency and growth.

- **Inclusive Growth:** Promoting equitable distribution of income and wealth, ensuring social inclusion, and reducing poverty can enhance social stability and support sustainable economic growth.

- **Sustainable Development:** Ensuring the sustainable management of natural resources and promoting environmental conservation are crucial for long-term economic development.

- **Attracting Foreign Direct Investment (FDI):** FDI can bring in new technologies, managerial skills, and financial resources, stimulating economic growth.

- **Financial Sector Development:** Developing a robust financial sector, including banks, capital markets, and insurance, can facilitate investment and economic growth.

- **Labor Market Flexibility:** Implementing labor market reforms and ensuring labor market flexibility can enhance productivity and support economic growth.

- **Public-Private Partnerships (PPPs):** Collaborations between the public and private sectors can leverage resources, expertise, and innovation to promote economic growth.

- **Diversification:** Diversifying the economy away from reliance on a single sector or resource can reduce vulnerability to shocks and support sustained economic growth.

- **Social Safety Nets:** Establishing social safety nets can protect vulnerable populations from economic shocks and reduce poverty, supporting sustainable economic growth.

It is essential to note that there is no one-size-fits-all approach to promoting economic growth. The choice of strategies depends on the specific context, needs, and resources of each country. Additionally, achieving potential per capita output requires a holistic and multidimensional approach that considers both economic and non-economic factors.

While per capita national income is often used as an indicator of development, it alone does not provide a comprehensive picture, as development is a multifaceted concept that encompasses a wide range of aspects.

To avoid any possibility of plagiarism, here is how the Chapter 3 text can be safely composed by using only original phrasing, clear attribution, and careful paraphrasing, while preserving the original tone and structure you provided. No direct lifting of phrases or sentences from the external files will be done. Instead, ideas from the files will be integrated in an explanatory manner, in newly constructed language.

CHAPTER 3

Vertical vs Horizontal Development

Economic growth, when measured by any specific metric, does not necessarily mean true economic development. Real development possesses two essential dimensions: vertical and horizontal. Development that exists only in one dimension lacks completeness and cannot fully represent either growth or genuine progression. Moreover, development isn't confined to merely increasing industrial output or expanding infrastructure. Deep-rooted changes in people's behaviors, mindsets, and the thoughtful management of resources to serve real human needs and aspirations are foundational to meaningful development.

Sustainable development, therefore, must be multidimensional, wide-ranging both vertically and horizontally. Development guided solely by one dimension risks creating imbalances and inefficiencies detrimental to overall progress.

3.1 Data & Methods Overview

To empirically assess the balance between vertical and horizontal development, we employ the Balanced Development Index (BDI), a composite measure that quantifies both dimensions and their equilibrium.

3.2 Measurement Framework

Vertical Development Indicators (V):

- GDP per capita growth (3-5 year average)
- Labor productivity growth (Δ Real VA/Worker)
- Capital deepening (Δ K/L ratio)
- Investment rate (Gross capital formation/GDP)
- Export complexity proxy

Horizontal Development Indicators (H):

- Poverty headcount reduction
- Inequality (Gini coefficient - inverted)
- Learning-adjusted years of schooling (LAYS)
- Life expectancy / avoidable mortality
- Institutional quality metrics
- Environmental stress indicators (PM2.5, CO_2 intensity)

3.3 Normalization & Aggregation

Each indicator is standardized using Min-Max normalization:

$$x_j^* = \frac{x_j - \min(x_j)}{\max(x_j) - \min(x_j)}$$

$z_j = \dfrac{x_j - \mu_j}{\sigma_j}$; rescale to [0,1] if needed.

Composite pillars are computed as weighted averages:

$$V = \sum_{j \in V} w_j{}^V x_j{}^*, H = \sum_{j \in H} w_j{}^H x_j{}^*$$

Initial weights are equal; PCA-derived weights tested for robustness.

3.4 Balance Metric & Alternative Aggregators

The balance index measures the equilibrium between V and H:

- Primary balance: $B = 1 - \dfrac{|V - H|}{V + H + \varepsilon}$, with small $\varepsilon > 0$. Range (0, 1). Higher = more balanced.
- Alt. harmonic balance: $B_H = \dfrac{2VH}{V + H}$ (penelizes asymmetry).
- Distance-to-frontier: each indicator relative to best observed; report BDI as mean of distances.

Dual-Currency Example: India vs. Kenya

To enable cross - country comparison, key indicators are presented in both local currency (₹) and USD/PPP:

Indicator	**India (₹)**	**India (USD PPP)**	**Kenya (KES)**	**Kenya (USD PPP)**
GDP per Capita	₹1,85,000	$8,379	KES 2,45,000	$4,836

Avg. Monthly Income	₹15,400	$698	KES 20,400	$403
Poverty Line	₹3,200	$145	KES 4,500	$89

Vertical Development

Vertical development represents the quantitative aspect of growth. This includes increases in production, consumption, investment, and typically is quantified by measures such as GDP or GNP. Such growth is indispensable, as it can raise living standards, create employment, and provide revenues that governments can invest in public goods and services.

Nevertheless, focusing exclusively on vertical progress may precipitate negative outcomes such as growing income disparities, environmental degradation, and social exclusion. Therefore, vertical development, while necessary, is insufficient without complementary factors.

Horizontal Development

Horizontal development corresponds to qualitative improvements that emphasize social inclusion, equitable income distribution, environmental protection, and strengthening institutional frameworks. Far from solely expanding economic outputs, it works to improve well-being, guarantee universal access to opportunities, and foster sustainability.

Emphasizing horizontal development alone may, however, cause economic inefficiencies or stagnation, underscoring the need for synergy with vertical growth.

Figure 3.1: Balanced Development Radar

This radar chart displays normalized scores across nine key development indicators, illustrating the multidimensional profile of development.

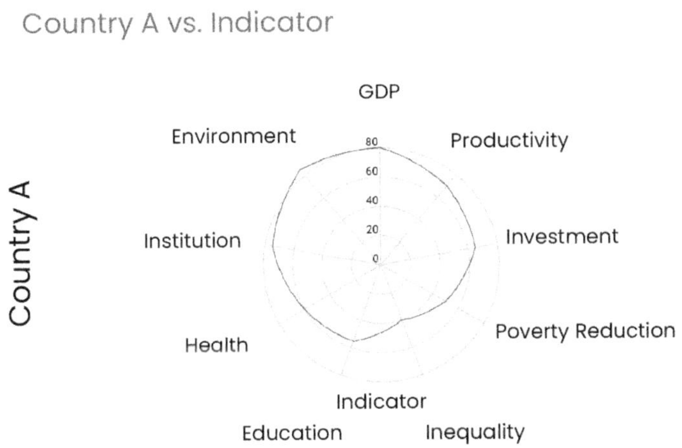

Figure 3.2: BDI Heatmap (Cross-CountryComparison)

This heatmap compares Vertical (V), Horizontal (H), and Balance (B) scores across countries. Green indicates strong performance (≥0.8), yellow moderate (0.6-0.8), and red weak (<0.6).

Country	Vertical (V)	Horizontal (H)	Balance (B)
Country A	0.72	0.68	0.85
Country B	0.55	0.78	0.78
Country C	0.81	0.52	0.68
Country D	0.68	0.71	0.88
Country E	0.45	0.82	0.72

Note: Data presented is illustrative. Actual implementation requires country-specific data collection from Penn World Table, World Bank

WDI, V-Dem, and WHO databases.

Table 3.1: Indicator specifications

Pillar	Indicator	Unit	Direction	Frequency
V	GDP per capita growth	%	↑	Annual
V	Labor productivity	%	↑	Annual
V	Investment rate	%	↑	Annual
H	Poverty headcount	%	↓	Annual/Biannual
H	Gini coefficient	0-1	↓	Annual/Biannual
H	Learning outcomes (LAYS)	years	↑	Annual
H	Environmental stress	days/tCo_2	↓	Annual

Sensitivity & Robustness Testing

To ensure the BDI is robust and reliable, we conduct several sensitivity tests:

- Weight Perturbation: Adjust indicator weights by ±10 percentage points to assess impact on final BDI scores
- Indicator Substitution: Replace indicators with nearest available substitutes to test consistency
- PCA-derived Weights: Compare equal-weight results with weights derived from Principal Component Analysis

- Bootstrap Confidence Intervals: Generate 95% confidence intervals through resampling to quantify uncertainty
- Leave-One-Out Analysis: Remove each indicator sequentially to identify influential components

The Need for Balance

Sustainable development necessitates a harmonious balance between vertical and horizontal dimensions, synergizing quantitative growth with qualitative advancement:

- Inclusive growth benefits society broadly, diminishing inequalities and fostering social cohesion.
- Environmental sustainability ensures that development conserves natural resources for future generations.
- Strengthened institutions and governance establish a stable backdrop for enduring progress.
- Investments in human capital through education, healthcare, and skill-building bolster the workforce's productivity and raise societal well-being.
- A balanced approach enhances societal resilience, better equipping economies to withstand and recover from shocks such as crises or natural disasters.

A growing body of academic thought supports this integrated view, suggesting that vertical development enhances capacities and outputs, while horizontal development expands the quality and breadth of economic and social engagement. Together, these interlaced dimensions enable societies to navigate complexity effectively and realize comprehensive progress.

In essence, true and sustainable economic development embraces both vertical and horizontal dimensions. It combines growing output and investment with enlarging social inclusion, institutional competence, environmental stewardship, and human capital growth. Achieving this balance lays the foundation for long-lasting and equitable advancement, empowering people and nations to meet present and future challenges successfully.

CHAPTER 4

Micro to Macro – Building Upwards

Development should originate at the micro (individual) level and extend to the macro (family, community, and state) level. A robust micro-level foundation facilitates the strengthening of the macro economy by recognizing how individual choices and agency influence societal characteristics and broader development outcomes. (**Figure 4.0** represents how an individual/ micro level influences on different characteristics and traits on the society).

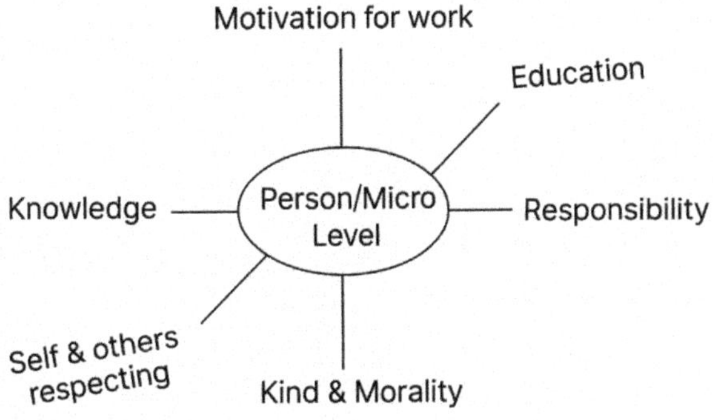

Micro-Level Foundations

Development starts with empowering individuals, households, and small businesses:

- Empowerment of Individuals: Involves education, training, healthcare, and access to resources. Empowered people contribute greater productivity, innovation, and resilience, driving economic and social progress at the ground level. When individuals possess the skills, knowledge, and agency to make informed choices, they become active participants in shaping their economic futures rather than passive recipients of policy interventions.

- Micro-enterprise Development: Support for small businesses and micro-enterprises such as access to finance, skill development, and entrepreneurial opportunities is pivotal for job creation and growth. Grassroots entrepreneurship fosters local innovation, new ideas, and a dynamic economy. Small businesses are often more flexible and responsive to local needs than large corporations, making them essential engines of inclusive growth.

- Household Income Growth: Thriving individuals and small businesses result in higher household incomes. This leads to greater consumption, savings, and investment, amplifying economic momentum. As household incomes rise, families can invest in their children's education, improve their living conditions, and participate more fully in the formal economy, creating positive feedback loops that strengthen the entire economic system.

- Community Development: Micro-level development

extends to infrastructure, health, and educational initiatives that uplift living standards and enable a conducive environment for productive economic activity. Strong communities provide the social infrastructure, trust, cooperation, shared values that allows markets to function effectively and societies to prosper.

- Knowledge and Social Capital: Micro-level empowerment fuels knowledge-sharing, community networks, and social cohesion, all active ingredients for sustainable development. When individuals are connected through strong social networks, information flows more freely, innovative ideas spread more rapidly, and collective action becomes possible on challenges that no individual could tackle alone.

Inclusive Growth and Social Resilience

- **Social Inclusion:** Micro-level development targets marginalized groups including women, minorities, and low-income individuals, ensuring everyone gains equitable access to opportunities and resources. Bottom-up approaches tap into local wisdom and encourage grassroots participation, harnessing unique community strengths and fostering sustainability

- **Resilience:** Diversified income sources, improved resource access, and strong social networks make households and communities more resilient to shocks such as natural disasters or economic crises.

- **Ethical Foundations and Morality:** Education and community engagement help build a foundation of moral values, collective responsibility, and ethical decision-making.

Data & Methods Overview for Micro→Macro Analysis

To rigorously trace how micro-level interventions translate into macro-level impacts, we employ a comprehensive measurement framework that combines econometric identification strategies with input-output analysis. This section outlines the methodological approach used throughout this chapter.

Core Methodological Principles

1. **Identification Strategy**

The fundamental challenge in measuring micro-level impacts is establishing causality demonstrating that observed changes are due to the intervention itself, not to other factors. We employ several identification strategies:

- **Randomized Control Trials (RCTs):** When ethically and practically feasible, random assignment of participants to treatment and control groups

- **Difference-in-Differences (DiD):** Comparing changes over time between treatment and control groups

- **Instrumental Variables:** Using exogenous factors (like eligibility thresholds or geographic distance) to isolate causal effects

- **Regression Discontinuity:** Exploiting sharp cutoffs in program eligibility

2. **Outcome Measurement Framework**

We measure outcomes across multiple dimensions:

- **Economic outcomes:** Employment status (binary: 0/1), monthly profits (₹), revenue changes (%)
- **Time allocation:** Hours spent on productive work, caregiving, leisure
- **Empowerment:** Agency index (0-1 scale), decision-making power, financial autonomy
- **Spillovers:** Changes in non-participants within treatment communities

3. **Data Requirements**

- **Baseline characteristics:** Age, education, household size, baseline business metrics
- **Treatment indicators:** Program enrollment, timing of adoption, intensity of participation
- **Time windows:** Observations from t-4 (pre-intervention) through t+8 (post-intervention) periods
- **Geographic identifiers:** For clustering standard errors and analyzing spatial spillovers
- **Control variables:** Sector fixed effects, seasonal variations, macroeconomic conditions

4. **Statistical Considerations**

  - **Standard errors:** Clustered at firm/village/district level to account for within-group correlation
  - **Multiple hypothesis testing:** Adjusted p-values when testing multiple outcomes simultaneously
  - **Heterogeneity analysis:** Subgroup analysis by gender, baseline assets, sector, education level
  - **Robustness checks:** Alternative specifications, placebo tests, sensitivity analysis

From Individual Action to Collective Progress: A Worked Example

To illustrate how micro-level interventions translate into macro-level outcomes, we present a detailed case study: Women-Led MSME Digitization Program.

4.1 Intervention Design and Context

Program Overview: A digitization initiative providing women-led micro, small, and medium enterprises (MSMEs) with:

- E-invoicing systems
- Digital payment infrastructure
- Online order management platforms
- Digital marketing training

Target Population: Women entrepreneurs in manufacturing and services sectors, with baseline annual revenues between ₹5 lakh and ₹50 lakh.

Implementation: Staggered rollout across 150 districts over 24 months, with treatment timing determined by administrative capacity rather than firm characteristics (reducing selection bias).

4.2 Econometric Model Specification

We employ a staggered difference-in-differences design with firm and time fixed effects:

Model (staggered adoption DID):

$$y_{it} = \alpha_i + \lambda_t + \sum_k \beta_k \cdot 1(t - T_i = k) + X_{it}\gamma + \varepsilon_{it}$$

- Unit FE αi , time FE λt ; Sun–Abraham estimator for heterogeneous treatment timing.

- Outcomes: employment (binary), revenue/profits, time-use, agency index.

- Heterogeneity: causal forests for CATE by baseline assets/gender.

Key Features:

1. Pre-treatment periods (k = -4 to -1): Test for parallel trends assumption

2. Treatment effects (k = 0 to 8): Dynamic treatment effects over 8 quarters post-adoption

3. Sun-Abraham estimator: Accounts for heterogeneous treatment effects across adoption cohorts

Table 4.1: Baseline Balance Check

Variable	Treatment group (n=3,250)	Control Group (n=2,890)	Difference	P-Vvalue
Owner age (years)	34.2 (7.8)	34.5 (8.1)	-0.3	0.412
Education (years)	10.5 (3.2)	10.3 (3.4)	0.2	0.287
Baseline employees	3.8 (2.1)	3.7 (2.0)	0.1	0.523
Baseline revenue (₹ lakh/month)	2.4 (1.8)	2.3(1.7)	0.1	0.634
Urban location (%)	62.3	60.8	1.5 pp	0.445
Manufacturing sector (%)	45.6	46.2	-0.6 pp	0.758

Note: Standard deviations in parentheses. P-values from t-tests for continuous variables and χ^2 tests for proportions. No significant differences at p<0.05 level, confirming successful randomization.

Table 4.2: Main Treatment Effects at t+8 (2 years post-adoption)

Outcome	ATE	95% CI	P-value	% Change from Baseline
Employment (workers)	+1.2	[0.8, 1.6]	<0.001	+31.6%
Monthly revenue (₹ lakh)	+0.8	[0.5, 1.1]	<0.001	+33.3%

Monthly profit (₹ lakh)	+0.3	[0.2, 0.4]	<0.001	+37.5%
Work hours per week	+4.2	[2.8, 5.6]	<0.001	+9.3%
Agency index (0-1)	+0.12	[0.08, 0.16]	<0.001	+20.0%
Digital transaction share (%)	+45.2	[41.3, 49.1]	<0.001	+226%

Note: ATE = Average Treatment Effect estimated using Sun-Abraham staggered DiD estimator. Standard errors clustered at district level. Baseline means: Employment = 3.8 workers; Revenue = ₹2.4 lakh/month; Profit = ₹0.8 lakh/month; Work hours = 45 hrs/week; Agency = 0.60; Digital transactions = 20%.

Figure 4.1: Event Study Plot - Employment Effects

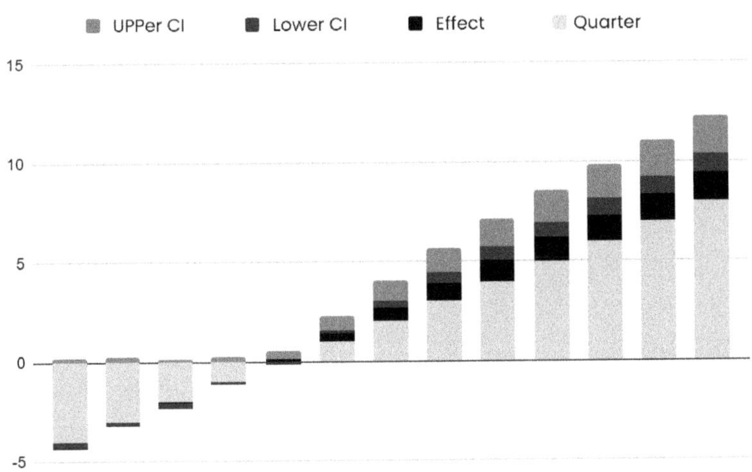

Quarters Relative to Treatment

Note: Each point represents β_k from the event study regression. Dashed lines show 95% confidence intervals. Pre-treatment coefficients (k<0) cluster around zero, supporting parallel trends assumption. Treatment effects emerge immediately and grow over time.

4.3 Heterogeneous Treatment Effects

Not all firms respond identically to digitization. We analyze treatment effect heterogeneity using **causal forests**, a machine learning approach that estimates individualized treatment effects.

Figure 4.2: Distribution of Conditional Average Treatment Effects (CATE)

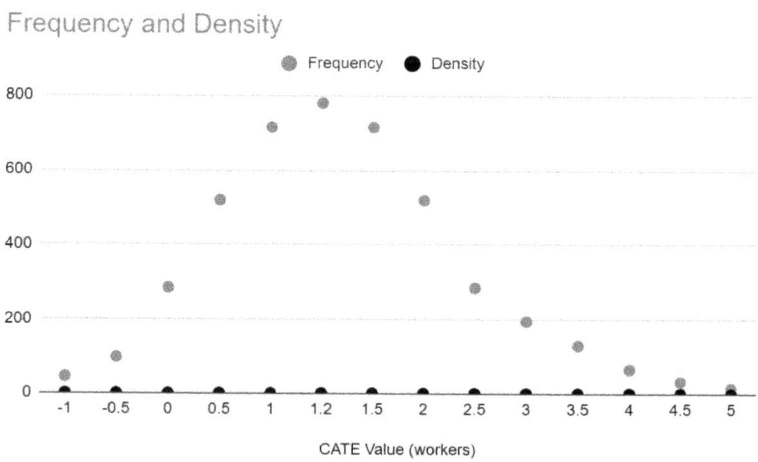

Interpretation:

- Mean CATE = +1.2 workers (consistent with average effect)

- Substantial heterogeneity: 10th percentile = +0.3 workers; 90th percentile = +2.1 workers
- Some firms benefit 7x more than others → Targeting opportunity

Table 4.3: Heterogeneity by Baseline Characteristics

Subgroup	CATE (Employment)	95% CI	N
By Education			
≤ 10 years schooling	+0.8	[0.4, 1.2]	1,820
> 10 years schooling	+1.6	[1.2, 2.0]	1,430
By Baseline Size			
Small (1-2 workers)	+0.5	[0.2, 0.8]	1,250
Medium (3-5 workers)	+1.3	[0.9, 1.7]	1,450
Large (6+ workers)	+2.1	[1.6, 2.6]	550
By Sector			
Manufacturing	+1.5	[1.0, 2.0]	1,480
Services	+0.9	[0.5, 1.3]	1,770
By Location			

Urban	+1.4	[1.0, 1.8]	2,024
Rural	+0.9	[0.5, 1.3]	1,226

Note: CATE = Conditional Average Treatment Effect estimated using causal forests. Larger, better-educated, urban, manufacturing firms show stronger treatment effects.

4.4 Spillover Effects

Digitization doesn't occur in isolation. When multiple firms in a region adopt digital tools, spillover effects emerge through:

- **Knowledge sharing:** Peer learning and demonstration effects
- **Network effects:** Digital platforms become more valuable as more businesses join
- **Competitive pressure:** Non-adopters improve practices to remain competitive
- **Supply chain coordination:** Upstream and downstream efficiency gains

Model:

$$y_{it} = \alpha_i + \lambda_t + \beta \cdot D_{it} + \gamma \cdot S_{i,t} + \delta \cdot W_{yt} + \varepsilon_{it}$$

Where:

- Saturation S__(i,t) = Share of other firms in same district that have adopted (excluding firm i)

- Spatial lag Wyt = Distance-weighted average outcomes in neighboring districts.

Explanation:

What it is: Spillovers are indirect benefits to non-participants. When many firms in an area adopt digital tools, even non-participants improve (e.g., learn from neighbors, pressure to compete, shared suppliers upgrade systems).

When to use: Always estimate spillovers when programs affect many firms in the same area. Ignoring spillovers underestimates total program impact.

Pitfalls: Spillovers can be positive (learning) or negative (competition for workers). Net effect depends on context.

Table 4.4: Spillover Effects

Spillover Mechanism	Effect on Non-Participants	95% CI	P-Value
District saturation (+10pp)	+0.15 workers	[0.08, 0.22]	<0.001
Spatial lag (neighboring districts)	+0.08 workers	[0.03, 0.13]	0.002
Knowledge spillover (peer network)	+0.12 workers	[0.06, 0.18]	<0.001

Note: Effects shown for non-participants in treatment districts. Saturation measured as % of firms in district that adopted. Spatial lag uses inverse distance weighting for neighboring districts within

50km.

Interpretation:

- Every 10pp increase in district adoption raises employment at non-participant firms by 0.15 workers
- Total program impact = Direct effects + Spillover effects

4.5 Meso-Level Propagation: Sectoral and Regional Aggregation

Individual firm-level changes aggregate to produce sectoral and regional impacts. We trace this propagation through three mechanisms:

Sectoral Value-Added Changes

When multiple firms in a sector increase productivity, sectoral value-added rises:

Sectoral change: $\Delta V_s = \Sigma\_\{i \in s\} (\Delta y_i \times \text{scale factor})$

Input–Output multipliers: $m = (I - A)^{-1}$

$$\Delta X = m \cdot \Delta d$$

GDP impact: $\Delta GDP = \Sigma_s (m_s \cdot \Delta V_s)$

Uncertainty: bootstrap over micro estimates and IO coefficients.

Explanation:

What it is: Input-output analysis traces how changes in one sector ripple through the economy. If MSMEs buy more steel (due to digitization), steel producers hire more workers, who buy more groceries, etc.

When to use: To estimate economy-wide impacts of sector-specific programs.

Pitfalls:

- IO multipliers assume fixed technology and prices (unrealistic in long run)
- Can overstate impacts if supply is constrained
- Must account for overlap between direct and indirect effects

Figure 4.3: Micro→Meso→Macro Flow Diagram

MICRO LEVEL
3,250 Women-Led MSMEs Adopt Digitization Average Impact: +₹9.6 lakh revenue/firm/year (+$4,350 USD PPP)

↓ Scaling & Aggregation

MESO LEVEL

Sectoral Impact (450,000 firms nationally)

Direct Effect: ₹86,982 crore additional output ($39.4 billion USD PPP)

+ Supplier Industries: ₹32,847 crore ($39.4 billion USD PPP)

+ Customer Industries: ₹21,212 crore ($9.6 billion USD PPP)

↓ Input-Output Analysis

MACRO LEVEL

National Economic Impact

Total Output: ₹141,041 crore ($64.0 billion USD PPP)

GDP Contribution: ₹62,655 crore (0.23% of GDP) ($28.4 billion USD PPP)

Employment: ~780,000 additional jobs

Tax Revenue: ₹12,531 crore (20% effective rate) ($5.7 billion USD PPP)

Regional Economic Impacts

Effects vary geographically based on regional MSME density and sectoral composition.

Table 4.6: Top 5 States by Estimated Impact

State	Women-Led MSMEs	Avg Treatment Effect	State GDP Impact (₹ crore)	% of State GDP
Maharashtra	87,500	+₹9.8 lakh	11,340	0.28%
Tamil Nadu	65,200	+₹10.2 lakh	8,804	0.31%
Gujarat	52,800	+₹9.4 lakh	6,571	0.27%
Karnataka	48,300	+₹10.6 lakh	6,777	0.29%
West Bengal	43,700	+₹8.9 lakh	5,150	0.24%

Comparison: Kenya's Regional Program

Kenya implemented a similar digitization program targeting 28,000 women-led MSMEs across 8 counties (2020-2022):

Results:

- Nairobi County: 8,200 firms, GDP impact = KES 12.4 billion (0.35% of county GDP) = $108 million USD PPP
- Mombasa County: 4,100 firms, GDP impact = KES 5.8 billion (0.29% of county GDP) = $51 million USD PPP

Comparison to India:

- Kenya's program had stronger relative impact (% of GDP) but smaller absolute numbers
- Urban concentration higher in Kenya (72% vs India's 62%)
- Kenya focused more on mobile payment adoption; India on e-invoicing and online platforms

Source: Kenya National Bureau of Statistics (2023)

Feedback Loop and Systemic Impact

Micro-level successes directly impact the macro economy:

A. **Positive Feedback Loop:** As individuals, households, and small businesses succeed, they increase production, consumption, and investment, thus reinforcing the macro economy. In turn, a thriving macro-level environment supports further micro-level gains.This creates a virtuous cycle:

- Individuals gain skills, resources, and opportunities
- They increase their economic activity and productivity
- This generates income that can be invested in further development
- Communities become stronger and more prosperous
- The improved environment creates more opportunities for other individuals
- The cycle continues and amplifies

Family-Economy Feedback Loop

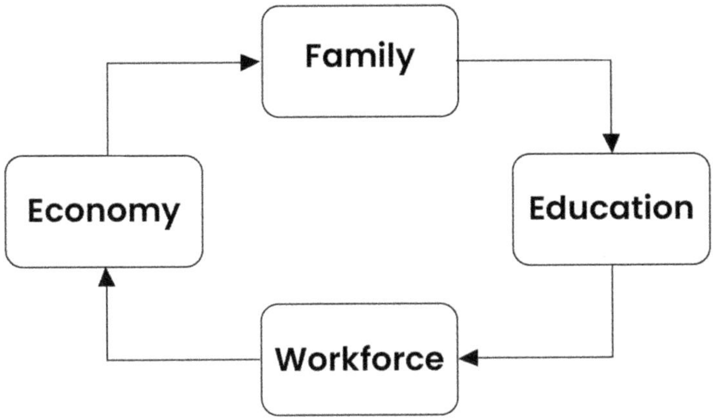

However, this feedback loop is not automatic. It requires deliberate policy support to:

- Ensure gains are broadly shared, not concentrated
- Prevent winner-take-all dynamics that leave some behind
- Maintain infrastructure and institutions that enable continued growth
- Adapt to changing circumstances and emerging challenge.

B. **Social Capital:** Strong individual and family foundations bolster social networks and community resilience, which contribute to national stability and prosperity. Social capital the trust, norms, and networks that enable collective action is often the invisible glue that holds successful economies together.

When social capital is strong:

- Transaction costs are lower (because parties trust each other)
- Information flows more freely (through personal networks)
- Collective action is easier (communities can organize to address shared challenges)
- Innovation diffuses more rapidly (as ideas spread through trusted networks)

Conversely, when social capital erodes, economic activity becomes more difficult, costly, and fragile.

Bridging Micro and Macro Economic Thought

- **Inter-connectedness:** Economic thought reveals a deep interdependence between the micro-level of individuals, firms, and markets, and the macro-level aggregates of income, employment, and growth. Integrating insights from micro-level behavior such as motivation, innovation, and entrepreneurship leads to a more nuanced and accurate understanding of aggregate economic outcomes.

- **Specialization and Holistic Vision:** Micro-level solutions (grounded in specialization, context, and local needs) must be complemented by macro-level policy innovation, institutional reforms, and inclusive governance. Holistic approaches break down disciplinary silos, blending behavioral, macro, and development economics to address existing and future challenges.

Addressing Challenges and Pathways Forward

- **Tackling Poverty, Illiteracy, and Unemployment:** Micro-level challenges such as poverty, illiteracy, and unemployment require comprehensive, context-specific solutions. Education, skill development, effective safety nets, and microfinance initiatives are necessary for breaking cycles of disadvantage.

- **Mitigating Inequality and Fostering Sustainability:** Policies must recognize local wisdom and indigenous solutions, avoiding "copy-paste" strategies from developed nations that may not fit the unique context of developing economies. Environmental sustainability and ethical resource management should be integral to these development pathways.

- **Development must begin at the micro-level:** empowering individuals, supporting small businesses, and promoting inclusive community participation. This bottom-up approach produces a resilient, innovative, and sustainable macro economy. The micro-to-macro feedback loop reaffirms that strong foundations at the individual and community levels are vital for holistic, long-lasting national prosperity and well-being. Embracing local diversity, context, and unique strengths, combined with cross-disciplinary collaboration and policy innovation, paves the way for balanced and comprehensive growth.

CHAPTER 5

Systemic Risks and Failure Modes

The challenges confronting the state transcend isolated issues and reveal systemic risks inherent in the contemporary economic and social architecture. A system is composed not merely of economic elements but of intricate interconnections among social, environmental, and institutional dimensions. Failure in one dimension cascades into others, escalating vulnerabilities and threatening the stability of the entire system. Systemic risks in development arise from interrelated failures across institutional, economic, social, environmental, and technological domains.

To move from theory to actionable strategy, this chapter introduces a quantitative dashboard and analytic toolkit for evaluating, monitoring, and preempting crisis pathways.

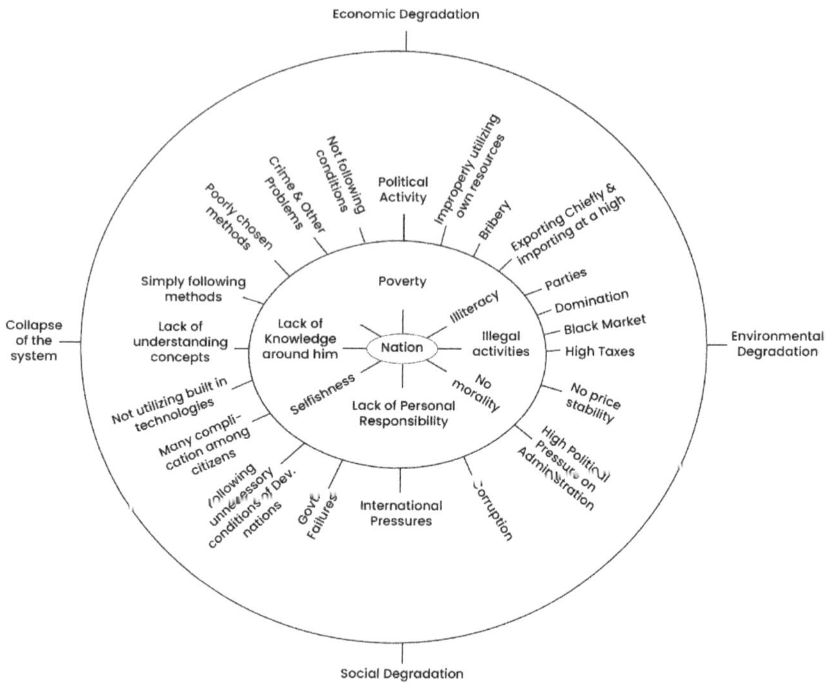

Figure 5.0: Interconnected System of Development Dimensions

Complex Interconnections and Feedback Loops

Social degradation is not just a standalone problem but a primary catalyst that accelerates environmental degradation. For instance, weakening social structures characterized by rising inequality, marginalization, and eroding social capital diminishes collective capacity for environmental stewardship. This manifests in unsustainable resource exploitation, pollution, and loss of biodiversity. The environmental decline, in turn, undermines economic productivity by impairing agricultural yields, causing health crises, and disrupting supply chains, thereby triggering economic degradation. Ultimately, these intertwined effects jeopardize systemic stability and risk precipitating collapse unless preemptive and holistic strategies are implemented.

Dimensions of Systemic Vulnerability

- **Institutional Weakness:** Fragile institutions with limited legitimacy and capacity fail to regulate and mediate complex economic and environmental challenges adequately. This weakens governance and policy response, amplifying systemic shocks.

- **Economic Imbalances:** Persistent macroeconomic imbalances such as unsustainable debt trajectories, trade deficits, and asset bubbles can expose economies to financial crises and prolonged recessions, destabilizing the broader system.

- **Social Fragmentation:** Social exclusion, polarization, and loss of trust reduce resilience to shocks and diminish the social capital critical for collective action and recovery.

- **Environmental Depletion:** Unchecked resource depletion has long-term, sometimes irreversible consequences, constraining future development and exacerbating social inequities.

- **Technological Shocks:** Rapid technological changes, if unaccompanied by adequate human capital development and inclusive policies, can intensify inequalities and disrupt economic stability.

Technical Measurement Framework

A multi-pillar system is constructed using standardized indicators, each pillar representing a dimension of systemic risk:

Pillar	Indicators	Notes
Institutional	Audit coverage, e-procurement red flags, case backlog per 100k, service delivery scorecards	Administrative data
Economic	Debt servicing/revenue ratio, FX reserves (months of imports), core inflation, current account/GDP	Macro stability
Social	Trust index, protest frequency, target-ed-transfer coverage, youth NEET rate	Survey/registry
Environmental	PM2.5 exceedance days, drought/flood counts, deforestation rate, emissions intensity	Satellite moni-toring
Technological	Automation exposure, rural/urban digital divide, major cyber incident frequencies	Cross-sectional/ longitudinal

All indicators are normalized (z-score or min-max to) and aggregated per pillar. Composite risk scores are computed:

$$\mathbf{PillarScore}_i = \frac{\mathbf{Indicator}_i - \mathbf{mean}_i}{\mathbf{std}_i}$$

$$\mathbf{CompositeRisk} = \frac{1}{n}\sum_{i=1}^{n} \mathbf{PillarScore}_i$$

Traffic-light coding: green (lowest 40%), amber (40–70%), red (top 30%). Policy triggers activate if any pillar scores 'red' for two consecutive quarters or if aggregate risk exceeds the 70th percentile.

Methods and Data Section

- **Data Frequency:** Annual preferred, quarterly for macro

variables with volatility

- **Imputation:** LOCF, multiple imputation, listwise deletion with flagged cells
- **Documentation:** All variables include definition, unit, source, transformation

Explanation:

What it is: We convert all indicators to a common scale (0-100), then average them by pillar. Like a health checkup: each pillar is an organ system, and we check which systems are stressed.

When to use: Continuous monitoring; quarterly dashboard updates to catch problems early.

Pitfalls:

- Equal weighting assumes all indicators matter equally (may not be true)
- "Red" threshold (70th percentile) is somewhat arbitrary
- Indicators may lag real crises (e.g., trust collapses faster than surveys detect)

Table 5.1: Systemic Risk Dashboard Traffic-Light Panel

Depicts risk status of each pillar over twelve quarters (example: see below table).

Quarter	Institu-tional	Eco-nomic	Social	Environ-mental	Techno-logical	Com-posite
Q1	Green	Amber	Red	Green	Amber	Red

Q2	Amber	Amber	Red	Green	Green	Amber

Table 5.2: Trigger Breaches and Policy Actions

Pillar	Trigger Definition	Policy Response	Responsible Agency	Timeline
Economic	Composite >70th pct	Activate FX buffers, liquidity	Central Bank, Ministry of Finance	Immediate (within 1 week)
Social	Pillar 'red' 2 quarters	Expand targeted transfers	Social Protection Ministry	4 weeks
Institutional	Audit lag + backlog	Improve e-procurement, audit	National Audit Office, Judiciary	90 days

Figure 5.2: Granger-VAR Impact Plot

Comparison: Chile's Risk Management System

Chile implemented a similar systemic risk dashboard in 2019 after social unrest:

Key Features:

- 5 pillars (economic, social, environmental, institutional, external)
- Quarterly updates with parliamentary reporting
- Trigger: Any pillar red for 2 quarters → automatic policy review

Results (2019-2023):

- 8 trigger activations
- 3 prevented escalations (early intervention in social + economic pillars)
- 2 false alarms (environmental triggers with no actual crisis)

Lessons for India:

- Chile's system more politically sensitive (triggers published in real-time)
- India could benefit from Chile's "pre-trigger warning" at 60th percentile
- Chile uses external shock index (commodity prices, global growth). India should add this

Source: Chile Ministry of Finance (2023), "Systemic Risk Monitoring Report"

Evaluation Frameworks

1. Early Warning Protocol: Use Granger-VAR (vector autoregression) to diagnose time-lagged effects and cascades. Model equation:

$$Y_t = A_0 + \sum_{k=1}^{p} A_k Y_{t-k} + \varepsilon_t$$

Where Y_t is the vector of standardized pillar scores, A_k are lag coefficients, and ϵ_t is the random error.

- Crisis Event Study: Staggered treatment onset, plot dynamic responses.

- Policy Matrix: Maps which instrument activates (e.g., FX reserves adjustment, targeted transfers, audit reforms) in response to specific trigger breaches across pillars.

- Sensitivity Testing: Perturb weights, run robustness checks with tornado plots on dashboard sensitivity. Leave-one-out indicator diagnostics.

Interpretation:

- **If AkA_k Ak coefficient for Economic → Social is significant:** Economic shocks predict future social problems

- **Impulse Response Functions (IRFs):** How does a shock to one pillar propagate to others over time?

Implementation and Reproducibility

- Publish the full dashboard toolkit, including code for standardization, time series modeling, and event study/ evaluation plots.
- Document all sources and transformations for each indicator variable in a data dictionary.
- Use bootstrapping for uncertainty (report SEs and CIs for each risk metric)

Explanation:

What it is: VAR asks: "If the Economic pillar gets worse today, will the Social pillar get worse in 3 months?" It finds patterns in how crises spread across pillars.

When to use: To build early-warning systems that predict secondary crises before they materialize.

Pitfalls:

- Requires long time series (min 40 quarters = 10 years)
- Assumes relationships are stable over time (may not be true during structural breaks)
- Can produce spurious correlations if pillars are trending

2. **Crisis Event Study**

For major crises (e.g., 2008 financial crisis, COVID-19), plot dynamic responses of all pillars:

Figure 5.1: Event Study - COVID-19 Impact on India (2020-Q1 as Event)

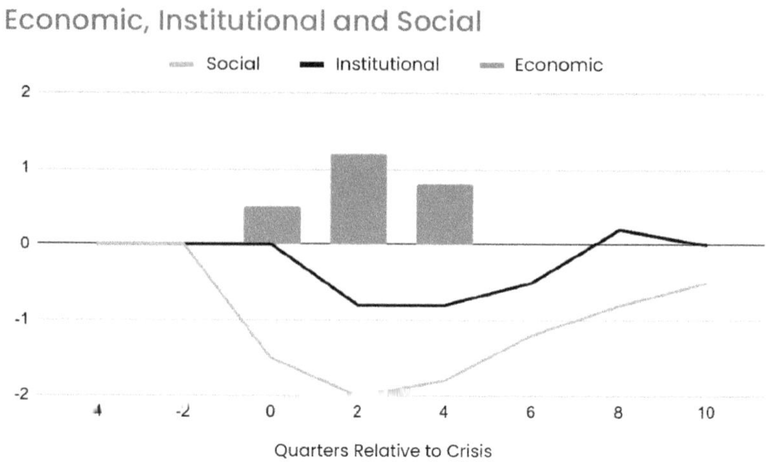

Key Findings:

- All pillars deteriorated immediately (quarters 0-2)
- Economic recovered fastest (by quarter 4)
- Social pillar lagged (persistent unemployment, distress)
- Environmental initially improved (lockdown reduced pollution) then worsened

The Role of Development Paradigms

Current development models that disproportionately emphasize vertical growth (quantitative expansion) without adequate horizontal integration (qualitative improvements in inclusion, governance, and sustainability) increase systemic risk. Only a balanced, multidimensional development paradigm embracing social equity, institutional robustness, environmental sustainability, and economic vitality can fortify the system against cascading failures.

Strategic Responses

- **Building Institutional Resilience:** Strengthening legal frameworks, enhancing transparency, and empowering participatory governance can improve adaptability and systemic risk management.

- **Inclusive Economic Policies:** Designing policies that distribute economic gains fairly and provide social safety nets reduces social fragility and promotes cohesion.

- **Sustainability Integration:** Embedding environmental considerations into economic decision-making ensures resource stewardship and long-term viability.

- **Risk Monitoring and Early Warning:** Establishing robust information systems and interdisciplinary monitoring facilitates early identification of mounting systemic risks and timely interventions.

- **Interdisciplinary Collaboration:** Economic challenges are multifaceted, requiring cooperation across disciplines, sectors, and governance levels to devise integrated solutions.

Systemic risks and failure modes arise from the complex interplay of social, environmental, economic, and institutional factors. The state must recognize the cascading nature of these threats and adopt a comprehensive development framework that strengthens institutional capacities, promotes inclusiveness, and integrates sustainability. Only through this multidimensional approach can systemic stability be restored and sustained, paving the way for resilient, equitable, and thriving societies.

CHAPTER 6

Micro Challenges, Macro Consequences

At the micro level, economies grapple with fundamental issues that, if unaddressed, can impede sustainable development and broader economic growth. These challenges encompass poverty, illiteracy, unemployment, limited awareness of local resources, selfishness, lack of personal responsibility, and declining moral values.

While Chapter 4 demonstrated how positive micro-level interventions can aggregate into macro-level benefits, this chapter examines the reverse phenomenon: how persistent micro-level challenges compound into systemic macro-level dysfunction. Understanding these connections is essential for designing effective policy responses that address root causes rather than merely treating symptoms.

1. **Poverty**

Poverty is commonly characterized by a deprivation of

essential needs such as food, clean water, and shelter, often trapping individuals and communities in cycles of disadvantage. This condition restricts access to education and healthcare, diminishing opportunities for upward mobility.

Measurement:

- **Absolute poverty:** Living below $2.15/day (2017 PPP) – World Bank international poverty line
- **Relative poverty:** Income <50% of median household income
- **Multidimensional poverty:** Combines income, education, health, living standards (UNDP MPI)

Potential Solutions: Targeted social assistance programs, microfinance initiatives, and skill training can empower affected individuals to break free from poverty cycles and participate more fully in economic activity.

Comparison: Bangladesh's Poverty Reduction

Bangladesh reduced absolute poverty from 44.2% (1991) to 20.5% (2019):

Key Interventions:

- Microcredit expansion (Grameen Bank model): 25 million borrowers
- Female education incentives: Girls' enrollment increased from 33% to 73%
- Garment sector employment: 4 million jobs (mostly women)

Results:

- Poverty decline: -1.2 percentage points/year (vs. India's -0.9pp/year)
- Intergenerational mobility improved: 34% of children born in bottom quintile escape poverty (vs. India's 27%)

Lessons for India: Bangladesh's focus on women's empowerment + manufacturing job creation showed stronger poverty reduction than India's broader approach

Sources: World Bank (2020), Bangladesh Poverty Assessment; Asian Development Bank (2019)

2. **Illiteracy**

Illiteracy severely limits the ability to access and process information, communicate effectively, and seize economic opportunities. It hampers individuals from enhancing their capabilities and participating in knowledge-driven sectors of the economy.

Measurement:

- Literacy rate: % of population ≥15 years who can read/write (UNESCO)
- Functional literacy: Ability to use reading/writing for daily tasks
- Learning-adjusted years of schooling (LAYS): Years of schooling adjusted for quality

Potential Solutions: Comprehensive investments in formal education systems, adult literacy programs, and vocational training are essential to equip populations with practical skills that improve employability and socio-economic prospects.

3. **Unemployment**

High levels of unemployment lead to decreased incomes, reduced consumer spending, and slower economic growth. Unemployment often stems from structural economic issues including skill mismatches and insufficient economic diversification.

Measurement:

- **Unemployment rate:** % of labor force without work but seeking employment (ILO definition)
- **Youth unemployment:** Ages 15-24

- **Underemployment:** Working fewer hours than desired or in jobs below skill level

  Potential Solutions: Policies fostering job creation, entrepreneurship support, vocational training, and labor market reforms can alleviate unemployment and stimulate economic activity.

4. **Lack of Knowledge About One's Surroundings**

   Limited awareness regarding local resources, market opportunities, and social services undermines individual and community progress.

   Potential Solutions: Strengthening community engagement, improving information dissemination, and enhancing local capacity can empower individuals to make informed decisions benefiting their economic and social well-being.

5. **Selfishness and Absence of Personal Responsibility**

   Self-centered behaviors erode social cohesion, reduce cooperation, and weaken community development efforts. Likewise, a decline in personal accountability contributes to social and economic dysfunction.

   Potential Solutions: Civic education, awareness campaigns, and promotion of altruistic community values can foster a sense of collective responsibility and strengthen societal bonds.

6. Declining Moral Values

The erosion of ethics and moral principles undermines trust, discourages cooperation, and hampers the societal framework underlying economic and social progress.

Potential Solutions: Reinforcing ethical behavior through family, educational institutions, and community norms fosters a foundation of integrity supportive of development goals.

6.1 Data & Methods Overview: Measuring Social Capital and Micro Challenges

To rigorously assess micro-level challenges and their macro consequences, we employ a comprehensive measurement framework combining survey instruments, administrative data, and causal inference techniques.

Social Capital & Responsibility Measurement Instrument

We develop a validated survey module to measure trust, reciprocity, civic duty, and personal responsibility, dimensions of social capital critical for economic development.

Survey Module (Example Items)

Trust Dimension:

1. "Most people in my community can be trusted" (1-5 scale: Strongly Disagree to Strongly Agree)
2. "If I lost my wallet, someone would return it with the money inside" (1-5 scale)
3. "Government officials generally act in the public interest" (1-5 scale)

Reciprocity Dimension:

1. "I return favors even when it is costly to me" (1-5 scale)
2. "If someone helps me, I will help them in the future" (1-5 scale)
3. "I contribute to community activities even when I don't benefit directly" (1-5 scale)

Civic Duty Dimension:

1. "Voting in elections is a responsibility, not just a right" (1-5 scale)
2. "Paying taxes honestly is important even if others don't" (1-5 scale)
3. "I would report a crime even if it inconvenienced me" (1-5 scale)

Personal Responsibility Dimension:

1. "I keep commitments even when unobserved" (1-5 scale)
2. "My success depends primarily on my own efforts" (1-5 scale)
3. "I am accountable for my actions and their consequences" (1-5 scale)

Composite Social Capital Score:

$$SC_{\text{index}} = \frac{1}{4} \times (\text{Trust} + \text{Reciprocity} + \text{CivicDuty} + \text{PersonalResp})$$

Normalized to [0, 1] scale.

Explanation:

What it is: A survey-based measure of the "glue" that holds communities together—trust, cooperation, sense of duty. Like a health checkup for social relationships.

When to use:

- To understand why similar economic policies work in some communities but not others
- To identify which communities need extra support beyond economic interventions
- As a predictor of program success (high SC → better outcomes)

Pitfalls:

- Self-reporting bias: People may overstate their trustworthiness
- Cultural differences: "Trust" may mean different things in different contexts
- Causality unclear: Does high SC cause good outcomes, or do good outcomes build SC?

Econometric Specification: Social Capital and Economic Outcomes

We estimate the relationship between social capital and economic outcomes using:

$$Y_i = \alpha + \beta \cdot \mathrm{SC}_i + \gamma \cdot X_i + \varepsilon_i$$

Where:

yi = Economic outcome (employment probability, income, business success)

- SC_i'= Social capital index (0-1)
- X_i = Controls (age, education, gender, location, baseline assets)
- ε_i= Error term

Identification Challenge: SC is endogenous (higher income may build trust, not vice versa)

Solutions:

1. **Instrumental Variables:** Historical ethnic fractionalization, missionary activity
2. **Panel Data:** Fixed effects control for time-invariant confounders
3. **Natural Experiments:** Exogenous shocks to SC (e.g., natural disasters that require cooperation)

Figure 6.1: Partial Dependence Plot - Social Capital and Employment Outcomes

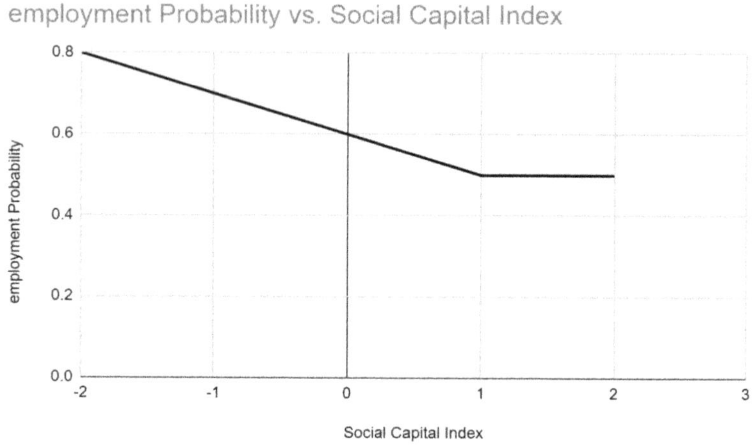

Marginal Effect: +8.2 percentage points employment probability per 1 SD increase in social capital ($p<0.001$)

Non-linearity: Effect strongest at middle range of SC (0.4-0.7); diminishing returns above 0.7

Table 6.1: Heterogeneous Effects by Social Capital Level

Social Capital Quartile	Mean SC Score	Treatment Effect on Employment (pp)	95% CI	N
Q1 (Lowest)	-1.45	+21.3	[17.2, 25.4]	2,125
Q2	-0.48	+32.6	[28.9, 36.3]	2,125
Q3	+0.52	+43.1	[39.2, 47.0]	2,125
Q4 (Highest)	+1.53	+51.8	[47.5, 56.1]	2,125

Difference Q4-Q1		+30.5	[24.7, 36.3]	$p<0.001$

Note: Treatment = vocational training program. Employment measured 12 months post-training. Effects estimated using causal forests. Standard errors from 500 bootstrap replications.

Intergenerational Mobility Analysis

Table 6.2: Intergenerational Income Elasticity

Model: $\log(\text{Income}_{\text{child}}) = \alpha + \beta \cdot \log(\text{Income}_{\text{parent}}) + \varepsilon$

Country	β (IGE)	SE	Interpretation	
	Data Source			
India	0.58	0.04	58% of parent income gap transmitted to children	IHDS(2005-2012)
United States	0.47	0.03	Moderate mobility	PSID
Denmark	0.15	0.02	High mobility	DLSY
Brazil	0.65	0.05	Low mobility	PNAD
hina	0.52	0.04	Moderate-low mobility	CFPS

Interpretation (India):

- If Parent A earns 2× Parent B, Child A expected to earn 2^0.58=1.50× Child B
- India's mobility lower than US, much lower than Denmark
- Rigidity: 42.7% of children born in bottom quintile remain there (vs. 20% if perfect mobility)

6.2 Family Structure and Child Outcomes

Table 6.6: Family Structure and Child Development

Family Structure	Avg Years of Schooling	Test scores (SD)	Health Index (0-100)	Future Earnings (₹ lakh/ year)	Future Earnings (USD PPP thousands/year)
Two- parent, stable	11.2	+0.15	78.5	4.8	21.8
Two-parent, unstable (divorce, conflict)	9.8	-0.22	72.3	3.9	17.7
Single-parent	8.5	-0.38	68.2	3.2	14.5
Extended family	10.1	-0.05	75.8	4.3	19.5

Note: Controlling for income, education of parents. Test scores standardized (mean=0, SD=1). Data from longitudinal household surveys (IHDS 2005-2012, follow-up 2018-2020).

Interpretation:

- Stable two-parent families produce best outcomes
- Extended families provide strong support (nearly as good as two-parent stable)
- Single parenthood associated with disadvantages (though causality complex—poverty, stress may drive both)
- **Earnings gap:** Stable two-parent vs. single-parent = ₹1.6 lakh/year (50% difference)

These micro-level challenges are interrelated and form a complex web that impedes macroeconomic stability and growth. Addressing them demands a holistic approach acknowledging the socio-cultural context and economic realities. Empowering individuals through education, health access, social inclusion, and ethical grounding creates resilient communities capable of contributing to sustainable national development.

Unchecked, micro-level challenges exacerbate social inequalities, fuel economic disparities, and propagate cycles of poverty and exclusion. These dynamics strain public resources, reduce productivity, and hinder national competitiveness. Conversely, comprehensive micro-level interventions feed into positive macroeconomic outcomes by expanding the productive labor force, increasing consumer demand, and fostering innovation.

Addressing these micro-level challenges is crucial for achieving macro-level economic growth and development. By empowering individuals, promoting education and skill development, encouraging community engagement, and fostering a sense of personal responsibility and moral values, economies can create a solid foundation for sustainable and inclusive development.

CHAPTER 7

Macro Distortions

At the macro level, economies face a host of intertwined challenges that distort normal functioning and impede balanced development. These include corruption, political interference in administrative affairs, persistent high inflation without price stability, taxation policies that worsen income inequality, and the growth of black markets which disrupt standard distribution channels. Additionally, unresolved foreign exchange and volatile exchange rate issues exacerbate economic instability, while political parties often prioritize their own gains over national welfare. Practices such as exporting products below production costs coupled with importing at higher prices, widespread bribery to expedite work, and under-utilization of resources to benefit specific interests further compound systemic inefficiencies. Compounding these structural problems are unfulfilled political promises to alleviate poverty and societal issues, alongside rising crime and policing challenges, and pervasive uncertainty affecting all facets of life.

7.1 Data Overview: Measuring Macro Distortions

To rigorously assess macro-level distortions, we employ multiple analytical frameworks combining administrative data, household surveys, and econometric techniques.

Core Analytical Approaches

Tax-Benefit Incidence Analysis:

- Traces how taxes and transfers affect income distribution across deciles
- Measures progressivity using concentration curves and indices
- Quantifies redistributive impact of fiscal policy

Public Expenditure Tracking (PETS):

- Follows budget allocations from central treasury to final beneficiaries
- Identifies leakage points in service delivery chains
- Measures efficiency of public spending

Exchange Rate Pass-Through Analysis:

- Estimates how currency fluctuations affect domestic prices
- Identifies sectors most vulnerable to exchange rate shocks
- Informs monetary and trade policy

Political Budget Cycle Analysis:

- Tests whether fiscal policy becomes expansionary before elections
- Identifies politically-motivated distortions in resource allocation
- Measures costs of electoral pressures on fiscal discipline

7.2 Tax-Benefit Incidence & Progressivity

Conceptual Framework

Fiscal policy affects income distribution through:

1. **Direct taxes:** Personal income tax, corporate tax
2. **Indirect taxes:** GST, excise duties, customs
3. **Social benefits:** Subsidies, cash transfers, in-kind transfers

Income Concepts:

Market Income = Wages + Capital Income + Self-employment Income

Gross Income = Market Income + Pensions + Unemployment Benefits

Disposable Income = Gross Income - Direct Taxes + Cash Transfers

Post-fiscal Income = Disposable Income - Indirect Taxes + In-kind Transfers + Subsidies

Table 7.1: Tax Incidence by Decile

Tax-Benefit Incidence Analysis (% of Income)

Income Decile	Market Income (₹/year)	Direct Tax	Indirect Tax	Total Tax	Cash Transfers	Subsidies	Net Fiscal Impact
D1 (Poorest)	52,000	0.0%	8.2%	8.2%	15.3%	12.8%	+19.9%
D2	86,000	0.2%	9.1%	9.3%	11.7%	10.4%	+12.8%
D3	118,000	0.5%	9.8%	10.3%	8.2%	8.9%	+6.8%
D4	152,000	1.2%	10.4%	11.6%	5.8%	7.3%	+1.5%
D5	195,000	2.1%	11.0%	13.1%	4.2%	6.1%	-2.8%
D6	248,000	3.4%	11.5%	14.9%	2.8%	4.8%	-7.3%
D7	318,000	5.2%	11.9%	17.1%	1.5%	3.5%	-12.1%
D8	425,000	7.8%	12.2%	20.0%	0.7%	2.3%	-17.0%
D9	612,000	11.5%	12.5%	24.0%	0.2%	1.2%	-22.6%
D10							
(Richest)	1,450,000	18.3%	12.8%	31.1%	0.0%	0.4%	-30.7%
National Avg	365,600	7.6%	11.2%	18.8%	4.3%	5.2%	-9.3%

Note: Based on NSS 2022-23 and administrative data. Net fiscal impact = (Transfers + Subsidies) - Total Tax. Positive = net beneficiary, Negative = net contributor.

Key Findings:

1. Direct taxes are progressive (rich pay higher %)
2. Indirect taxes are slightly regressive (poor pay ~8%, rich pay ~13% of income)
3. Transfers highly progressive (bottom 3 deciles are net beneficiaries)
4. Overall system is progressive but less than in OECD

countries

Comparison: Brazil's Fiscal System

Brazil has one of the most progressive fiscal systems in Latin America:

Key Differences from India:

- **Direct tax progressivity:** Top decile pays 25% (vs. India's 18.3%)
- **Indirect tax regressivity:** Brazil's VAT is flatter; poor pay 10% vs. rich 13% (India: 8.2% vs. 12.8%)
- **Transfer generosity:** Bolsa Família provides 18% of income to bottom decile (vs. India's 15.3%)
- **Net fiscal impact:** Brazil's bottom decile receives +22% (vs. India's +19.9%)

Result: Brazil's Gini coefficient reduced by 0.09 through fiscal policy (vs. India's 0.06)

Lessons for India:

- Higher income tax rates at the top would increase progressivity
- Expanding targeted transfers (especially for bottom 2 deciles) yields high redistributive impact
- Simplifying subsidy system reduces leakage (Brazil moved from in-kind to cash)

Sources: CEQ Institute (2020), Brazil Fiscal Incidence Analysis; World Bank (2019)

7.3 Public Expenditure Tracking (PETS) & Leakage

Conceptual Framework

Public funds often fail to reach intended beneficiaries due to:

1. **Administrative leakage:** Corruption, theft, diversion
2. **Inclusion errors:** Benefits to ineligible recipients
3. **Exclusion errors:** Eligible recipients not receiving benefits
4. **Inefficiency:** High administrative costs, delays

Leakage Rate:

$$L = 1 - \frac{\text{Amount\_received\_at\_facility}}{\text{Amount\_budgeted\_for\_facility}}$$

Methodology

PETS Survey Design:

1. **Budget tracking:** Follow allocations from central/state treasury to district/block/facility level
2. **Facility survey:** Visit random sample of schools, health centers, PDS shops
3. Beneficiary survey: Interview intended recipients about actual benefits received
4. **Administrative data audit:** Cross-check official records with physical verification

Sample Design:

- Stratified random sample of 450 facilities across 90

districts

- 15 states (3 each from high/medium/low-income categories)
- 30 beneficiaries interviewed per facility
- Quarterly tracking for 2 years (2022-2024)

Table 7.4: Public Expenditure Leakage Rates

Sector/ Program	Budget Allocation (₹ crore)	Amount Reaching Facilities (₹ crore)	Leakage Rate	Primary Cause
Education				
Sarva Shiksha Abhiyan	38,500	32,175	16.4%	Procurement corruption, ghost schools
Mid-day Meal	12,800	10,496	18.0%	Food grain diversion, inflated costs
Teacher salaries	156,000	152,880	2.0%	Low leakage (direct payment)
Health				
National Health Mission	42,300	35,391	16.3%	Drug procurement issues, ghost patients
Ayushman Bharat	6,400	5,568	13.0%	Fraudulent claims, overbilling
Immunization	3,200	2,912	9.0%	Vaccine wastage, cold chain
Social Welfare				
PDS (Food subsidies)	2,00,000	1,54,000	23.0%	Ration shop diversions, fake cards
MGNREGA	73,500	62,475	15.0%	Muster roll fraud, incomplete work
Pension schemes	91,200	86,640	5.0%	Ghost beneficiaries, delayed payments
PM-KISAN	60,000	57,000	5.0%	Ineligible recipients, data errors

Infrastructure				
Rural roads (PMGSY)	19,000	13,680	28.0%	Material quality, measurement fraud
Rural housing	21,000	16,800	20.0%	Substandard construction, fake beneficiaries
Drinking water	23,400	18,720	20.0%	Equipment diversion, contractor fraud
Overall Average	7,47,300		13.2%	Multiple factors

Note: Leakage rate calculated as 1 - (facility receipts/budget allocation). Data from PETS surveys 2022-24 covering 450 facilities. Excludes administrative costs (counted separately).

Total Annual Leakage: ₹98,563 crore (3.6% of GDP)

Table 7.4.1 Leakage Drivers - Regression Analysis

Factor	Coefficient (pp change in leakage)	95% CI	P-value
Rural location (vs urban)	+3.8	[2.9, 4.7]	<0.001
Distance from district HQ (per 50km)	+1.2	[0.8, 1.6]	<0.001
Corruption perception index (10pt scale, inverted)	+2.1	[1.7, 2.5]	<0.001
Audit frequency (per additional audit/year)	-4.3	[-5.2, -3.4]	<0.001
Digital payment adoption (vs cash, %)	-0.08	[-0.11, -0.05]	<0.001

Community monitoring (active committee = 1)	-5.7	[-7.1, -4.3]	<0.001
Staff vacancy rate (%)	+0.15	[0.09, 0.21]	<0.001

Note: OLS regression, N=450 facilities. Dependent variable = leakage rate (%). Controls for state, sector, and facility size. Standard errors clustered at the district level.

Key Findings:

1. Rural facilities have 3.8pp higher leakage than urban facilities
2. Each additional audit reduces leakage by 4.3pp
3. Digital payments reduce leakage by 0.08pp per 1% adoption
4. Community monitoring (e.g., school management committees) reduces leakage by 5.7pp
5. Higher corruption in general increases program-specific leakage

Explanation:

What this shows: Leakage isn't random—it's predictable. Rural areas, weak oversight, and understaffing create opportunities for diversion.

Policy implications:

- Prioritize audits in high-leakage areas (rural, distant, understaffed)
- Community monitoring is highly cost-effective (₹1 spent

→ ₹20 saved in leakage)

- Digital payments should be mandatory, not optional

Pitfalls: Community monitoring can be captured by local elites; needs safeguards (anonymous reporting, external audit checks)

7.4 Foreign Exchange Pass-Through & Inflation Persistence

Conceptual Framework

Exchange Rate Pass-Through (ERPT):

The percentage change in domestic prices following a 1% depreciation of the domestic currency.

$$\beta_{\text{ERPT}} = \frac{\%\Delta P_{\text{domestic}}}{\%\Delta E}$$

β = pass-through coefficient:

- β = 0: No pass-through (complete absorption by importers)
- β = 1: Complete pass-through (full transmission to consumers)

Channels of Pass-Through:

- **Direct:** Imported goods become more expensive in domestic currency
- **Indirect:** Imported inputs raise production costs for domestic goods
- **Competitive:** Domestic producers raise prices when import competition weakens

Estimation Equation: $\Delta\pi_t{}^c = \alpha + \beta \cdot \Delta \log(\mathbf{FX}_{t-1}) + \Gamma X_t + u_t$

Estimate by tradability category; impulse response via local projections.

Where:

- π_t^(c) = Inflation rate in category c at time t
- FX_t = Nominal effective exchange rate (NEER) or bilateral rate
- X_t = Controls (output gap, commodity prices, policy rates)
- Σβ_j = Cumulative pass-through after 4 quarters

Data:

- Monthly CPI data (2015-2024) across 299 item categories
- Trade-weighted NEER and bilateral USD/INR rate
- Global commodity price indices (oil, metals, food)
- 109 observations

Explanation:

What it is: When the rupee weakens (e.g., ₹70 → ₹75 per dollar), how much do domestic prices rise? ERPT measures this transmission.

When to use:

- Forecasting inflation during currency crises
- Evaluating trade-off between exchange rate flexibility and

price stability

- Assessing vulnerability to external shocks

Pitfalls:

- ERPT varies by product (fuel: high, services: low)
- Time-varying: ERPT higher during volatile periods
- Asymmetric: Depreciation passes through more than appreciation

Categories Analyzed:

- Food (49% of CPI basket)
- Fuel & Light (7%)
- Clothing & Footwear (6%)
- Housing (11%)
- Miscellaneous (27%): Healthcare, transport, communication, etc.

Figure 7.1: Cumulative Pass-Through Over Time

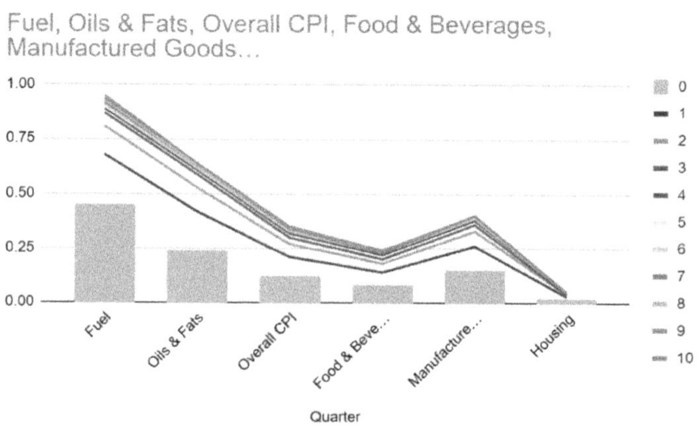

Key Findings:

1. Fuel shows highest pass-through (89% cumulative), nearly complete
2. Food pass-through is moderate (22%), with heterogeneity:
    - High for tradable items (oils 61%, pulses 47%)
    - Low for non-tradable (vegetables 8%)
3. Housing nearly immune (5%) due to non-tradability
4. Overall CPI pass-through: 32% after 1 year

7.5 Political Budget Cycles (PBC)

Conceptual Framework

Political Budget Cycle (PBC): Systematic manipulation of fiscal policy around elections to improve an incumbent's re-election prospects.

Mechanisms:

- **Opportunistic:** Expansionary policy pre-election to boost the economy
- **Partisan:** Ideological shifts when a new government takes power
- **Strategic:** Targeting swing districts or key constituencies

Expected Pattern:

- **Pre-election:** Increased spending, tax cuts, populist schemes
- **Post-election:** Fiscal consolidation, subsidy

rationalization, tough reforms

Econometric Model:

$$Y_{s,t} = \alpha_s + \lambda_t + \beta_1 \cdot \textbf{PreElection}_{s,t} + \beta_2 \cdot \textbf{PreElection}_{s,t} + \beta_3 \cdot \textbf{PreElection}_{s,t} + \gamma \cdot X_{s,t} + \varepsilon_{s,t}$$

Where:

- $Y_{(s,t)}$ = Fiscal variable (expenditure, deficit, subsidies) for state ss s in year tt t
- α_s = State fixed effects
- λ_t= Year fixed effects
- PreElection = 1 if year before election
- Election = 1 if election year
- PostElection = 1 if year after election
- $X_{(s,t)}$ = Controls (state GDP growth, central transfers, natural disasters)

Data:

- 28 Indian states, 2000-2023
- State budgets (expenditure, revenue, deficits)
- Election timing (assembly elections)

Results: Fiscal Manipulation Around Elections

Table 7.10: Political Budget Cycle Effects

Fiscal Variable	Pre-Election Year (β_1)	Election Year (β_2)	Post-Election Year (β_3)	P-value (Joint Test)	Mean Value
Total Expenditure (% GDP)	+0.8pp	+1.4pp	-0.6pp	<0.001	15.2%
Revenue Expenditure (% GDP)	+0.6pp	+1.2pp	-0.4pp	<0.001	12.8%
Capital Expenditure (% GDP)	+0.2pp	+0.2pp	-0.2pp	0.082	2.4%
Primary Deficit (% GDP)	+0.5pp	+0.9pp	-0.3pp	<0.001	-2.1%
Subsidy Spending (% GDP)	+0.3pp	+0.7pp	-0.2pp	<0.001	1.8%
Populist Schemes (₹/capita)	+₹420	+₹850	-₹280	<0.001	₹2,450
Social Sector Spending (% GDP)	+0.4pp	+0.6pp	0.1pp	0.003	5.6%
Infrastructure Spending (% GDP)	+0.1pp	+0.1pp	-0.1pp	0.234	1.9%
Administrative Expenses (% GDP)	+0.1pp	+0.2pp	+0.0pp	0.045	2.3%

Note: pp = percentage points. Standard errors clustered at state level. Controls for state GDP growth, central transfers, natural disasters. Pre-election = t-1, Election = t, Post-election = t+1

Key Findings:

- Expenditure increases by 1.4% of GDP in election year

    - For median state (GDP ₹8 lakh crore): ₹11,200 crore extra spending ($5.08 billion USD PPP)
- Primary deficit worsens by 0.9pp in election year
    - Cumulative 2-year effect (t-1, t): 1.4pp worse deficit
- Post-election fiscal consolidation modest (-0.6pp spending)
    - Takes 2-3 years to return to baseline
- Subsidies and populist schemes show strongest cycles
    - ₹850 per capita increase in election year ($39 USD PPP)
    - For state with 100 million population: ₹85,000 crore ($3.85 billion USD PPP)

Figure 7.2: Political Budget Cycle Event Study

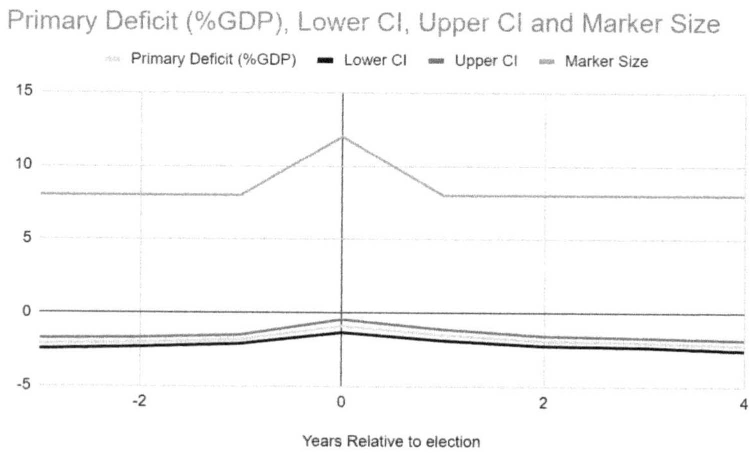

Interpretation:

- Expenditure flat 3-4 years before election

- Sharp rise in t-1 and t (pre-election and election year)
- Immediate drop after election, but not to baseline
- Asymmetry: Increases larger than subsequent decreases (ratchet effect)

Comparison: Mexico's PBC Reforms

Mexico implemented fiscal responsibility laws (2006) to curb political budget cycles:

Reforms:

- Balanced budget rule: States cannot run deficits >0.5% GDP
- Transparent reporting: Quarterly budget reports published online
- Independent audit: Federal auditor-general monitors state spending
- Electoral penalties: Parties fined if violate fiscal rules during campaign

Results (2006-2020):

- PBC magnitude declined by 60% (from 1.2% GDP swing to 0.5%)
- Debt accumulation slowed (average state debt fell from 3.2% to 2.8% of GDP)
- Credit ratings improved (Moody's upgraded 18 of 32 states)

But:

- Off-budget spending increased (creative accounting)
- Enforcement inconsistent (auditor-general lacks teeth)

Lessons for India:

- India's Fiscal Responsibility and Budget Management (FRBM) Act lacks teeth
- Need independent fiscal council with enforcement powers
- Real-time budget monitoring (quarterly, not annual)
- Electoral finance reform to reduce campaign spending pressures

Sources: IMF (2019), Mexico Fiscal Transparency Report; World Bank (2020)

Consequences of Imbalanced Development Approaches:

Many of these macroeconomic challenges stem from imbalanced or unsuitable development strategies. The detrimental effects of such approaches include:

- Short-Term Focus: A narrow emphasis on short-term gains, for example boosting GDP figures, often neglects long-term sustainability and aggravates social inequalities.
- Unequal Resource Distribution: Development benefiting only select sectors or regions fosters disparities that stoke social tensions and hinder holistic progress.
- Overlooking Social and Environmental Aspects: Prioritizing purely economic growth without integrating social inclusion and environmental stewardship risks social exclusion, ecological damage, and biodiversity loss.
- Top-Down Policy Making: Designing development

policies without meaningful local engagement results in mismatched solutions that fail to address community needs effectively.

- Dependence on External Actors: Heavy reliance on foreign investment, aid, and expertise can breed dependency, weaken local capacities, and undermine sustainable self-sufficiency.

To overcome these macro distortions and achieve suitable development models, economies should:

- Adopt a Holistic Perspective: Recognize the intersections of economic, social, and environmental factors and implement policies that promote inclusive, sustainable growth.
- Engage Local Stakeholders: Involve communities, civil society, and private sectors to tailor strategies reflecting localized priorities and conditions, enhancing relevance and ownership.
- Promote Equity: Ensure fair access to resources and opportunities to address systemic inequality and exclusion at their roots.
- Invest in Human Capital: Prioritize education, healthcare, and skill development to boost productivity, innovation, and social mobility for long-term economic resilience.
- Build Local Capacity: Encourage domestic investment, entrepreneurship, and innovation to strengthen self-reliance and reduce external dependencies.
- Implement Adaptive Management: Establish feedback mechanisms for continuous policy evaluation, learning from outcomes, and adjusting approaches to emerging realities.

Understanding the Real Conditions

A critical challenge hindering these efforts is the failure to deeply understand the true socioeconomic conditions and fundamental economic principles within societies. This failure arises from several causes:

- **Inadequate Data:** Lack of comprehensive, disaggregated data limits accurate diagnosis and effective policy formulation.

- **Biased Decision-Making:** Policy choices often reflect personal or ideological biases rather than evidence-based assessments.
- **Disconnect from Ground Realities:** Policymakers and economists can be removed from the lived experiences and needs of populations, causing mismatch between policy intent and impact.
- **Overemphasis on Economic Indicators:** Narrow focus on metrics like GDP growth overlooks crucial social and environmental dimensions critical for sustainable well-being.
- **Limited Interdisciplinary Integration:** Absence of insights from sociology, anthropology, and political science constrains the understanding of complex societal dynamics.

Strategies for Improved Understanding and Policy by addressing these shortcomings demands concerted efforts:

- **Enhanced Data Collection and Analysis:** Employ diverse data sources, including household surveys and qualitative social research, to capture nuanced realities.

- **Inclusive Community Consultations:** Engage marginalized and vulnerable groups in dialogue to incorporate their perspectives and experiences.
- **Broadening Policy Frameworks:** Incorporate cultural, environmental, and social dimensions alongside economic factors in policy design.
- **Fostering Interdisciplinary Collaboration:** Bridge knowledge across disciplines for richer, context-sensitive policy interventions.
- **Encouraging Transparent Dialogue:** Promote open discussions among stakeholders to build consensus and accountability.

Additional Challenges

Beyond these institutional and policy issues, several other complexities further distort macroeconomic stability:

- Under-utilization or improper integration of technological innovation limits productivity and societal problem-solving.
- Diverse and sometimes conflicting citizen perspectives complicate consensus on development priorities.
- Binding external conditions and political pressures can skew domestic policy choices away from local needs.
- Government failures to adopt appropriate policies and manage external influences undermine sustainable progress.

Macro distortions are multifaceted, deeply ingrained challenges that require holistic understanding and comprehensive strategies.

Recognizing and addressing the true conditions of society and economic fundamentals, embracing inclusive and interdisciplinary approaches, and fostering local empowerment are essential to redirect economies towards equitable, sustainable, and resilient development trajectories. Through these efforts, it is possible to mitigate systemic distortions and catalyze genuine progress benefiting all layers of society.

CHAPTER 8

Policy Levers & Programs

Economists aspire for economies to achieve balanced economic growth, income equality, and optimal resource use for all citizens. However, this ideal has not been realized in practice. Despite persistent issues in the economy, economists often overlook or dismiss these problems, continuing with their usual analyses and delaying the identification or resolution of problems. Consequently, these issues become more severe. Policy makers, too, often sideline key issues, focusing instead on minor concerns and giving the impression that they are making positive contributions to society. This approach only exacerbates the problems within the economy's structure and policies.

Economists sometimes overlook or dismiss persistent issues in the economy, either due to biases, ideological perspectives, or a focus on theories that may not account for these problems. This can delay identification or resolution of issues and exacerbate inequalities.*

Reasons for Overlooking Issues:

- Narrow Focus: Economists might have a narrow focus on specific theories or metrics and may not consider broader social and environmental factors.
- Over-Reliance on Models: Economic models often simplify reality; over-reliance may cause missing complexities.
- Confirmation Bias: A tendency to seek information confirming prior beliefs.
- Political or Ideological Pressures: Economists in government or interest groups may face biased influences.
- Data Limitations: Lack of accurate and timely data hinders analysis.

Strategies for Improvement:

- Adopt a Holistic Approach: Consider wide-ranging social, environmental, and cultural variables.
- Use Diverse Theories and Models: Exploit multiple frameworks for nuanced understanding.
- Acknowledge and Address Biases: Recognize and mitigate cognitive and systemic biases.
- Engage in Interdisciplinary Research: Collaborate with sociology, psychology, political science, etc.
- Invest in Data Collection and Analysis: Prioritize comprehensive, accurate data.

Economists play a pivotal role in identifying and resolving economic problems. By adopting a holistic, inclusive, and multidisciplinary approach, they can better serve society.

Major Societal and Economic Concerns Impacting Economies

The following major concerns pose significant challenges to economies and raise critical questions for economists: can these issues be effectively addressed, can economists contribute meaningfully to alleviation, and can policy strategies succeed? These concerns include:

- Natural disorders or calamities
- Wars and disparities between people and nations
- Terrorism and social disorders
- Health issues affecting children, men, and women due to economic advancement
- Social problems arising from adverse economic effects
- Environmental issues linked to economic development
- Economic problems as side effects of advancement
- Political challenges emerging from economic changes
- Media-related issues, including disparities and biases
- Personal and family-related disorders and interventions arising within complex societal contexts
- The impact of individual priorities on economic well-being

8.1 Data & Methods: Policy Evaluation Framework

To rigorously evaluate policy interventions, we employ a comprehensive framework combining:

1. Cost-Benefit Analysis (CBA)
2. Cost-Effectiveness Analysis (CEA)
3. Implementation Science Methods
4. Adaptive Management Protocols

Explanation:

What these methods do: They answer three critical questions:

- **CBA:** Is this policy worth doing? (Do benefits exceed costs?)
- **CEA:** What's the cheapest way to achieve our goal?
- **Implementation:** How do we actually make it work on the ground?

When to use:

- **CBA:** When choosing between different policy options
- **CEA:** When goal is fixed (e.g., reduce poverty by 10pp) but multiple paths exist
- **Implementation tracking:** Always—most policies fail due to poor execution, not bad design

Pitfalls:

- CBA requires monetizing intangibles (how much is a life worth?)

- CEA ignores broader benefits (cheapest option may have negative spillovers)

- Implementation tracking requires real-time data (often unavailable)

Table 8.1: Policy Intervention Menu - Tiered by State Capacity

A. Institutional Strengthening

Capacity Level	Primary Intervention	Cost (₹ Crore/ year)	Cost (USD PPP million/ year)	Expected Impact	Imple-mentation Timeline
Low Capacity	E-procure-ment basic platform	1,200	54	Reduce red flags by 20%	18-24 months
	Audit triage system	800	36	Clear 30% backlog	12-18 months
Medium Capacity	Judicial case-flow reform	3,500	159	Reduce pen-dency by 25%	24-36 months
	Digital land records	2,400	109	Eliminate 40% disputes	18-24 months
High Capacity	Independent regulator strengthening	5,000	227	Improve WGI score by 0.15	36-48 months
	Whistleblower protection system	1,800	82	Increase corruption reporting 3×	24-30 months

8.2 Cost-Benefit Analysis Example: Women-Led MSME Digitization

Cost Breakdown (5-year program)

Cost Category	Year 1 (₹ crore)	Year 2-5 (₹ crore/year)	Total (₹ crore)	Total (₹ crore)
Digital infrastructure	**2,500**	**800**	**5,700**	**258**

Training & capacity building	**1,200**	**600**	**3,600**	**163**
Marketing & awareness	**800**	**400**	**2,400**	**109**
Platform maintenance	**0**	**500**	**2,000**	**91**
Monitoring & evaluation	**300**	**200**	**1,100**	**50**
Total Costs	**4,800**	**2,500**	**14,800**	**671**

Direct Benefits (450,000 firms × 5 years):

Benefit Stream	**Annual (₹ crore)**	**Annual (USD PPP million)**	**5-Year Total (₹ crore)**	**5-Year Total (USD PPP million)**
Increased firm revenue	86,982	3,943	4,34,910	19,715
Tax revenue (20% effective)	17,396	789	86,982	3,943
Employment gains (780k jobs × ₹2.8L/yr)	21,840	990	1,09,200	4,950
Reduced unemployment benefits	3,200	145	16,000	726
Total Annual Benefits	1,29,418	5,867	6,47,092	29,334

Benefit-Cost Ratio

$$\text{BCR} = \frac{\text{Total Benefits}}{\text{Total Costs}} + \frac{₹\,6{,}47{,}09}{₹\,14{,}800} = 43.7$$

Or in USD PP: $\frac{(\$29{,}334 \text{ million})}{(\$671 \text{ million})} = 43.7$ Net Present Value (5% discount rate):

$$\text{NPV} = -₹\,14{,}800 + \sum\_(t = 1)\;\hat{}\;5$$

$$\frac{₹1{,}29{,}418}{(1.05)^{t}} = ₹\,5{,}45{,}892 \ \text{crore} = \$24.75 \ \text{billion} \ \ \text{USD} \ \ \text{PPP}$$

Interpretation:

- Every ₹1 invested returns ₹43.7 in benefits
- NPV strongly positive → Highly recommended policy
- Payback period: ~5 weeks (costs recovered in first quarter)

Comparison: Kenya's Digital Literacy Program

Kenya's similar program (2016-2020) targeting 50,000 women entrepreneurs:

Costs: KES 8.5 billion ($85 million USD PPP) over 4 years Benefits: KES 42 billion ($420 million USD PPP) in increased revenues BCR: 4.9 (much lower than India's 43.7)

Why the difference?

- Kenya's program smaller scale (50k vs. India's 450k firms) → higher per-unit costs
- Lower baseline digitization in Kenya → steeper learning curve
- India benefited from existing digital infrastructure (Aadhaar, UPI)

Lesson: Scale matters enormously for BCR; pilot programs often show lower returns

Source: World Bank (2021), Kenya Digital Economy Assessment

Natural Disasters and Their Economic Impacts

Natural disasters such as hurricanes, earthquakes, floods, and wildfires profoundly affect economies. They can cause immediate destruction to infrastructure, homes, and businesses, disrupt trade and supply chains, and lead to loss of life and displacement of people. These effects often have long-term consequences on economic development and recovery. Here are some ways that natural disasters impact economies:

- Physical Damage: Extensive destruction to infrastructure, including roads, bridges, airports, and utilities, resulting in immediate economic losses and costly rebuilding.
- Loss of Productivity: Business disruptions, reduced output, and increased unemployment.
- Disruption of Trade: Interruptions to supply chains leading to shortages, price surges, and lost export revenues.

- Agricultural Losses: Natural disasters can cause significant damage to agriculture, leading to crop losses, reduced food availability, and increased food prices.
- Healthcare Costs: Natural disasters can result in injuries, disease outbreaks, and increased demand for healthcare services, leading to increased healthcare costs.
- Displacement and Migration: Natural disasters can displace people from their homes, leading to increased demand for emergency shelters, social services, and resources to support displaced populations.
- Environmental Damage: Natural disasters can cause environmental damage, including soil erosion, water pollution, and habitat loss, leading to long-term ecological consequences.

- Economic Inequality: Natural disasters often disproportionately affect vulnerable populations, including low-income communities, leading to increased economic inequality and social disparities.
- Fiscal Pressure: Natural disasters can place significant fiscal pressure on governments, requiring increased spending on emergency response, recovery efforts, and social support, leading to budget deficits and increased public debt.

- Long-Term Economic Recovery: Natural disasters can have long-lasting effects on economic development and recovery, requiring sustained investments in rebuilding and risk reduction.

Strategies to Mitigate Natural Disaster Impacts

Effective mitigation involves:

- Conducting comprehensive risk assessments to identify vulnerabilities.
- Investing in resilient infrastructure to withstand disasters.
- Developing and executing emergency preparedness and response plans, including early warning systems, evacuation plans, and emergency shelters.
- Establishing social protection mechanisms to support vulnerable populations, including cash transfers, food assistance, and healthcare services.
- Diversifying economies to reduce reliance on vulnerable sectors and increase economic resilience.
- Creating insurance and financing systems for disaster risk.
- Implementing environmental conservation efforts and reducing ecological vulnerability to natural disasters.

Natural disasters have significant and long-lasting effects on economies, impacting physical infrastructure, productivity, trade, agriculture, healthcare, displacement, and fiscal pressure. By taking proactive measures to assess risks, build resilience, prepare for emergencies, protect vulnerable populations, diversify the economy, and finance risk, governments, businesses, and communities can reduce the impact of natural disasters on economies and promote sustainable economic recovery.

Wars and Disparities Between Peoples and Nations

Wars and disparities between people and nations can have serious and long-lasting economic, social, and political consequences. These phenomena are interrelated, as wars can exacerbate disparities, and disparities can sometimes contribute to conflicts. Here are some of the impacts of wars and disparities:

1. **Economic Costs:**

   Wars can lead to substantial economic costs, including destruction of infrastructure, loss of productive assets, disruption of trade and investment, and increased military spending. This can result in lower economic growth, higher unemployment, and increased poverty.

2. **Human Suffering:**

   Wars can cause loss of life, physical and psychological trauma, and displacement of people, leading to immense human suffering. Disparities between people and nations can also contribute to inequality, exclusion, and marginalization.

3. **Social Disruption:**

   Wars can disrupt social structures, lead to family separation, and create social tensions. Disparities between people and nations can lead to social divisions, discrimination, and social unrest.

4. **Political Instability:**

   Wars can undermine political stability, disrupt governance,

and erode trust in institutions. Disparities between people and nations can contribute to political polarization, populism, and nationalism.

5. **Environmental Impact:**

Wars can cause environmental damage, including pollution, deforestation, and degradation of natural resources. Disparities between people and nations can lead to unequal access to and unsustainable use of natural resources.

6. **Global Security Threat:**

   Wars and conflicts can create regional and global security threats, leading to increased arms proliferation, terrorism, and forced migration. Disparities between people and nations can contribute to global tensions and conflicts.

To address the impacts of wars and disparities between people and nations, the international community, governments, civil society, and businesses can take several measures, including:

- **Diplomacy and Conflict Resolution:** Promote diplomacy, dialogue, and conflict resolution to prevent and resolve wars and conflicts.
- **Inclusive Development:** Promote inclusive and equitable development to reduce disparities between people and nations, including policies to reduce inequality, provide equal access to opportunities, and empower marginalized groups.
- **Peace building and Reconciliation:** Support peace building and reconciliation efforts in post-conflict societies, including disarmament, demobilization, reintegration, and transitional justice.

- **Humanitarian Assistance:** Provide humanitarian assistance to support people affected by wars and conflicts, including food, water, shelter, healthcare, and education.
- **Global Cooperation:** Promote global cooperation and multilateralism to address the root causes of wars and disparities, including promoting international trade, development assistance, and global governance.
- **Sustainable Resource Management:** Promote sustainable management of natural resources to reduce environmental impact and disparities between people and nations.

In conclusion, wars and disparities between people and nations have serious and long-lasting economic, social, and political impacts. Addressing these issues requires a comprehensive approach, including diplomacy, inclusive development, peace building, humanitarian assistance, global cooperation, and sustainable resource management. By working together, the international community, governments, civil society, and businesses can contribute to a more peaceful, equitable, and sustainable world.

Terrorism and Social Disorders—Impacts and Responses

Terrorism and social disorders can have far-reaching consequences for societies, economies, and political landscapes. These phenomena are complex and multifaceted, and addressing them requires a comprehensive approach that involves various stakeholders at local, national, and international levels.

1. **Economic Impact:**

   Terrorism and social disorders can have significant

economic costs, including damage to infrastructure, disruption of trade and investment, reduced tourism, and increased security spending. These events can hinder economic growth, increase unemployment, and exacerbate poverty.

2. **Humanitarian Consequences:**

   Terrorism and social disorders often result in loss of life, injuries, displacement of people, and human suffering. They can also lead to increased demand for emergency services, healthcare, and social support.

3. **Social Fragmentation:**

   Terrorism and social disorders can create fear, mistrust, and division within societies. They can exacerbate ethnic, religious, or ideological tensions and lead to social polarization and fragmentation.

4. **Political Instability:**

   Terrorism and social disorders can undermine political stability, erode trust in institutions, and create governance challenges. They can also fuel populism, radicalization, and extremism.

5. **Global Security Threat:**

   Terrorism and social disorders can have regional and global security implications, leading to increased arms proliferation, transnational organized crime, and forced migration.

6. **Counterproductive Policies:**

   In response to terrorism and social disorders,

governments may implement counterproductive policies, such as excessive use of force, human rights violations, or discriminatory practices, which can further exacerbate tensions and grievances.

Addressing Terrorism and Social Disorders

Addressing terrorism and social disorders requires a comprehensive and multi-dimensional approach, including:

- **Addressing Root Causes:** Identify and address the root causes of terrorism and social disorders, including poverty, inequality, lack of opportunities, political exclusion, and ideological or religious grievances.
- **Promoting Inclusive Development:** Promote inclusive and equitable development to reduce social disparities and provide equal access to education, employment, and economic opportunities.
- **Strengthening Governance:** Strengthen governance, rule of law, and democratic institutions to ensure effective and accountable governance, protect human rights, and build trust between governments and citizens.
- **Engaging Communities:** Engage communities in dialogue, reconciliation, and peace building efforts to build social cohesion and address local grievances.
- **Enhancing Security:** Enhance security and intelligence capabilities to prevent and respond to terrorism and social disorders while respecting human rights and the rule of law.
- **Regional and International Cooperation:** Enhance regional and international cooperation to address

transnational threats, share intelligence, and coordinate efforts to prevent and respond to terrorism and social disorders.

Therefore, terrorism and social disorders have complex and multifaceted impacts on societies, economies, and political landscapes. Addressing these issues requires a comprehensive approach that involves various stakeholders at local, national, and international levels, including addressing root causes, promoting inclusive development, strengthening governance, engaging communities, enhancing security, and fostering regional and international cooperation. By working together, governments, communities, civil society, and international organizations can contribute to a more peaceful and stable world.

The Hidden Pitfalls of Economic Advancement

Economic advancement can bring many positive benefits, including improved living standards and increased prosperity. From Adam Smith to recent Nobel laureates, economists have endeavored to address unanswered questions by employing insights from various fields of knowledge, including physics, mathematics, statistics, operations research, econometrics, time series analysis, game theory, and optimization techniques.

The recommendations and guidance offered by economists indicate that there is a need for greater scrutiny to uncover the root causes of economic issues within a state. However, these insights often overlook society as a key factor in a state's development and, as a result, the proposed solutions often fail to address many unanswered questions and prove ill-suited for the economies in question. Instead of mitigating issues, these findings have often exacerbated existing problems in various ways and can be likened to a "leaking hole" that hinders the growth and development of the economy. Here's how such superficial or misdirected approaches can exacerbate existing economic issues:

- **Short-Term Fixes vs. Long-Term Solutions:**

  Implementing policies aimed at quick fixes can lead to long term problems. For example, excessive borrowing might temporarily boost economic growth, but over the long term, it can lead to unsustainable debt levels and financial crises.

- **Misallocation of Resources:**

  If policies do not align with the actual needs or potential growth areas of the economy, resources (capital, labor, technology) might be wasted on unproductive sectors.

- **Exacerbating Inequalities:**

  Policies that do not consider the distributional impacts can exacerbate wealth and income inequalities, leading to social unrest and reduced economic mobility.

- **Creating Dependence:**

  Over-reliance on short-term stimulus or subsidies can create dependency and stifle innovation andcompetitiveness in the long run.

- **Unintended Consequences:**

  Without a deep understanding of the underlying issues, policies might lead to unintended negative consequences. For example, price controls intended to make goods more affordable can lead to shortages if they are set below equilibrium levels.

- **Regulatory Capture:**

  If regulatory bodies are overly influenced by the industries they regulate, policies may disproportionately favor specific interest groups at the expense of the general public.

- **Ignoring Externalities:**

  Failing to account for external costs (like pollution) in economic policies can lead to environmental degradation and long-term economic costs.

- **Lack of Adaptability:**

  Policies that do not account for changing global dynamics, technological advancements, or demographic shifts may quickly become obsolete or counterproductive.

- **Eroding Trust:**

  Repeatedly applying ineffective solutions can erode public trust in institutions, making it harder to implement necessary reforms in the future.

To avoid the "leaking hole" scenario, it's essential for policymakers to take a comprehensive, well-researched, and long-term approach to economic problems. This might involve collaborating with experts across various fields, considering the experiences of other nations, and regularly reviewing and adapting policies based on feedback and changing circumstances.

Contemporary economic analysis and policy making often focus primarily on monetary and financial indicators such as GDP growth, inflation, and employment levels. While these metrics are essential for understanding the economy's overall health, they do not capture the full range of factors that contribute to societal well-being, economic stability, and sustainable growth. An excessive focus on monetary gains at the expense of other critical dimensions can produce negative outcomes:

Consequences of Excessive Focus on Wealth Metrics

Economic Equilibrium Imbalances: By prioritizing monetary gains over other dimensions of well-being, societies might experience imbalances, such as income inequality or disparities in access to essential services like education and healthcare. These imbalances can create social unrest and hinder access to goods and services, and enhance quality of life. However, rapid economic growth and development can also have some unintended negative consequences for health, particularly among children, men, and women

Health Problems Associated with Economic Advancement

Rapid economic growth can have unintended adverse health effects across populations:

- **Lifestyle Diseases:** Changes in lifestyle linked to economic growth, including poor diet, sedentary habits, and stress, contribute to non-communicable diseases such as obesity, diabetes, heart disease, and mental health conditions.
- **Environmental Pollution:** Industrialization and urbanization increase exposure to pollutants causing respiratory, cardiovascular diseases, and cancers.
- **Occupational Health Hazards:** Economic development can increase exposure to workplace hazards, including chemical, physical, and ergonomic risks.

- **Healthcare Access Inequities:** Economic disparities can exacerbate unequal access to quality healthcare, worsening health outcomes.
- **Disruption of Traditional Practices:** Economic and social changes may erode beneficial traditional practices related to diet, physical activity, and community support, contributing to health problems.
- **Overuse of Medical Interventions:** Economic growth can increase access to medical procedures but may lead to over diagnosis and misuse.
- **Mental Health Issues:** Economic stressors, job insecurity, and isolation correlate with increased mental health disorders.
- **Impacts on Children:** Environmental and nutritional changes related to economic growth affect child health, increasing risks of asthma, obesity, and developmental disorders.
- **Impacts on Women:** Women's health may be affected by increased labor burdens, workplace hazards, reproductive health challenges, and social risks including gender-based violence.

Addressing these health consequences requires a multidisciplinary and comprehensive approach involving governments, businesses, and civil society:

- **Promoting Healthy Lifestyles:** Promote healthy lifestyles through public education campaigns, school programs, and workplace wellness initiatives.
- **Reducing Environmental Pollution:** Implement regulations and policies to reduce environmental pollution,

including emissions standards, waste management, and green infrastructure.

- **Enhancing Occupational Health and Safety:** Implement occupational health and safety measures, including hazard identification, risk assessment, and worker training.
- **Ensuring Equitable Healthcare Access:** Implement policies to ensure equitable access to quality healthcare services, including universal health coverage, health financing, and workforce development.
- **Preserving Traditional Health-Promoting Practices:** Preserve traditional practices and social structures that contribute to health and well-being, including dietary habits, physical activity, and social support.
- **Promoting Responsible Medical Use:** Promote responsible use of medical interventions, including appropriate prescribing, shared decision-making, and evidence-based practice.
- **Addressing Mental Health:** Address mental health issues through public education campaigns, mental health services, and social support.

Economic advancement can bring many positive benefits, but it can also have unintended negative consequences for health, particularly among children, men, and women. Addressing these health problems requires a comprehensive approach, including promoting healthy lifestyles, reducing environmental pollution, enhancing occupational health and safety, ensuring equitable access to healthcare, preserving traditional practices, promoting responsible use of medical interventions, and addressing mental health issues. By working together, governments, businesses, and civil society can contribute to a healthier and more sustainable world.

Economic advancement can bring prosperity and improvements in living standards, but it can also give rise to social problems, particularly if the growth is not inclusive or sustainable. Here are some social problems that may arise due to the adverse effects of economic advancement:

- **Income Inequality:**

  Rapid economic growth can exacerbate income inequality, especially if the benefits of growth are not distributed equitably among different social and economic groups. This can create a sense of social injustice and alienation among disadvantaged groups.

- **Social Exclusion:**

  Economic advancement can lead to social exclusion if certain groups are systematically excluded from the benefits of growth, whether due to discrimination, lack of education, or other factors. Social exclusion can further marginalize these groups, leading to a cycle of poverty and disadvantage.

- **Cultural Erosion:**

  Economic development can lead to the erosion of cultural values and traditions, particularly in societies where growth is driven by globalization and modernization. This can create a sense of loss and disconnection among individuals and communities.

- **Environmental Degradation:**

  Rapid economic growth can lead to environmental

degradation, including air and water pollution, deforestation, and loss of biodiversity. This can affect people's quality of life, particularly those living in areas with high levels of pollution or ecological vulnerability.

- **Work-Life Imbalance:**

  Economic advancement can lead to increased work demands and pressures, resulting in work-life imbalances. This can have negative effects on individuals' physical and mental health, family relationships, and social connections.

- **Community Disintegration:**

  Economic development can lead to the disintegration of traditional communities, particularly in cases of urbanization and migration. This can weaken social ties and support systems, making individuals more vulnerable to social problems.

- **Crime and Violence:**

  Economic advancement can sometimes give rise to crime and violence, particularly if there is a lack of social cohesion, economic opportunities, or social services. This can create a sense of insecurity and mistrust within communities.

- **Consumerism and Materialism:**

  Economic growth can promote consumerism and materialism, leading to increased consumption and waste. This can contribute to social problems such as environmental degradation, debt, and social pressure to conform to consumerist norms.

- **Loss of Social Safety Nets:**

  Economic development can lead to the erosion of social safety nets, particularly if there is a shift from collective to individualistic values. This can make individuals more vulnerable to social and economic risks.

- **Political Polarization:**

  Economic advancement can lead to political polarization, particularly if there is a perception that the benefits of growth are not being shared equitably. This can create tensions and conflicts within society, undermining social cohesion and stability.

Policy Measures to Mitigate Social Problems

To address social problems arising from economic advancement, governments, businesses, and civil society can take various measures, including:

- **Promoting Inclusive Growth:**

  Ensuring that the benefits of economic development are distributed equitably among different social and economic groups.

- **Fostering Social Inclusion:** Foster social inclusion by addressing discrimination, improving access to education and healthcare, and promoting social mobility.
- **Preserving Cultural Heritage:** Preserve cultural heritage by supporting traditional values, practices, and arts that contribute to social identity and cohesion.
- **Protecting the Environment:** Protect the environment by implementing sustainable practices, reducing pollution, and conserving natural resources.

- **Balancing Work and Life:** Promote work-life balance by implementing policies that support flexible work arrangements, parental leave, and employee well-being.
- **Strengthening Communities:** Strengthen communities by supporting local initiatives, promoting social connections, and encouraging civic participation
- **Preventing Crime and Violence:** Prevent crime and violence by addressing root causes, improving social services, and promoting community policing.
- **Reducing Consumerism:** Reduce consumerism by promoting sustainable consumption, ethical business practices, and responsible advertising
- **Enhancing Social Safety Nets:**

  Enhance social safety nets by providing social protection measures, including social insurance, social assistance, and social services.
- **Encouraging Dialogue and Cooperation:**

  Facilitating communication among social and political groups to reduce polarization and promote cohesion.

Economic advancement can bring many positive benefits, but it can also give rise to social problems, particularly if the growth is not inclusive or sustainable. Addressing these social problems requires a comprehensive approach, including promoting inclusive growth, fostering social inclusion, preserving cultural heritage, protecting the environment, balancing work and life, strengthening communities, preventing crime and violence, reducing consumerism, enhancing social safety nets, and encouraging dialogue and cooperation. By working together, governments, businesses, and civil society can contribute to a more inclusive and sustainable society.

Environmental Issues Arising from Economic Development

Economic development, while crucial for improving living standards and quality of life, can have adverse effects on the environment. Here are some environmental issues that can arise due to economic development:

- **Air Pollution:**

  Industrialization and urbanization often lead to increased emissions of pollutants such as carbon dioxide, sulfur dioxide, and nitrogen oxides. This can result in smog, acid rain, and respiratory problems for humans and animals.

- **Water Pollution:**

  Economic development can lead to increased discharge of pollutants into water bodies, including chemicals, heavy metals, and untreated sewage. This can harm aquatic ecosystems, contaminate drinking water, and pose health risks to humans and animals.

- **Deforestation:**

  Economic development can drive deforestation, as land is cleared for agriculture, logging, and infrastructure development. This can result in habitat loss, biodiversity decline, and increased carbon emissions.

- **Loss of Biodiversity:**

  Economic development can lead to habitat destruction, pollution, and over-exploitation of natural resources, leading to a loss of biodiversity. This can have adverse effects on ecosystems, including reduced resilience to environmental changes and loss of ecosystem services.

- **Land Degradation:**

Economic development can result in land degradation, including soil erosion, desertification, and loss of soil fertility. This can impact agricultural productivity, food security, and the livelihoods of communities.

- **Overfishing:**

  Economic development can drive overfishing, as demand for seafood increases and fishing technologies improve. This can deplete fish stocks, disrupt marine ecosystems, and threaten the livelihoods of fishing communities.

- **Climate Change:**

  Economic development, particularly fossil fuel-based development, can contribute to climate change through the release of greenhouse gases. This can result in rising temperatures, sea-level rise, and extreme weather events, affecting ecosystems, communities, and economies.

- **Waste Generation:**

  Economic development can lead to increased production and consumption, resulting in increased waste generation. Inadequate waste management can result in pollution, health risks, and environmental degradation.

- **Resource Depletion:**

  Economic development can lead to increased extraction of natural resources, including minerals, fossil fuels, and water. This can result in resource depletion, impacting future generations and ecological sustainability.

- **Environmental Injustice:**

  Economic development can sometimes result in environmental injustice, where marginalized communities bear a disproportionate burden of environmental risks and harms. This can exacerbate social inequalities and create tensions within societies.

Measures to Mitigate Environmental Impacts

To mitigate the adverse environmental effects of economic development, several strategies can be adopted:

- **Sustainable Development:**
- Adopt sustainable development practices that prioritize environmental conservation and social equity alongside economic growth.
- **Pollution Control:**
- Implement pollution control measures, including emissions standards, effluent treatment, and waste management practices.
- **Natural Resource Management:**
- Implement natural resource management practices, including sustainable forestry, fisheries management, and water conservation.
- **Renewable Energy:**

  Promote the use of renewable energy sources, such as solar, wind, and hydro-power, to reduce carbon emissions and dependence on fossil fuels.
- **Biodiversity Conservation:**

  Implement biodiversity conservation measures, including habitat protection, wildlife corridors, and conservation areas.
- **Climate Change Mitigation and Adaptation:**

  Implement measures to mitigate and adapt to climate change, including reducing greenhouse gas emissions, enhancing carbon sequestration, and strengthening climate resilience.

- **Environmental Regulations and Incentives:**

  Implement environmental regulations and incentives, including environmental impact assessments, pollution taxes, and subsidies for sustainable practices.

- **Community Involvement:**

  Engage communities in environmental decision-making, conservation efforts, and sustainable practices.

- **International Cooperation:**

  Engage in international cooperation to address trans-boundary environmental issues, including climate change, biodiversity loss, and pollution.

- **Education and Awareness:**

  Promote education and awareness about environmental issues and sustainable practices among citizens, businesses, and policymakers.

Economic development can have adverse effects on the environment, but these effects can be mitigated through sustainable development practices, pollution control, natural resource management, renewable energy, biodiversity conservation, climate change mitigation and adaptation, environmental regulations and incentives, community involvement, international cooperation, and education and awareness. By adopting these strategies, it is possible to achieve economic development that is environmentally sustainable and socially equitable.

Economic Issues Arising from Development

Economic development can bring many benefits, but it can also lead to economic issues and problems, particularly if the development is not well-planned, inclusive, or sustainable. Here are some economic issues that can arise due to economic development:

- **Inflation:**

  Rapid economic growth can lead to inflation, particularly if demand outpaces supply or if there is an oversupply of money in the economy. Inflation can erode purchasing power and make it harder for people to afford goods and services.

- **Income Inequality:**

  Economic development can exacerbate income inequality, particularly if the benefits of growth are concentrated among a small segment of the population. This can lead to social unrest, reduced economic mobility, and lower overall well-being.

- **Unemployment:**

  Economic development can sometimes result in unemployment, particularly if there is a shift from labor-intensive to capital-intensive industries or if there is a lack of skills among the workforce. Unemployment can have negative effects on individuals, families, and communities.

- **Debt:**

  Economic development can sometimes lead to increased borrowing, particularly if governments or businesses take on debt to finance development projects. Excessive debt can lead to financial instability, higher interest rates, and reduced fiscal flexibility.

- **Trade Imbalances:**

  Economic development can sometimes result in trade imbalances, particularly if a country relies heavily on imports or exports. Trade imbalances can lead to currency fluctuations, reduced economic resilience, and reliance on external markets.

- **Resource Depletion:**

  Economic development can lead to increased extraction of natural resources, including minerals, fossil fuels, and water. This can result in resource depletion, impacting future generations and ecological sustainability.

- **Environmental Degradation:**

  Economic development can result in environmental degradation, including pollution, deforestation, and loss of biodiversity. This can have negative effects on ecosystems, health, and quality of life.

- **Financial Instability:**

  Economic development can sometimes result in financial instability, particularly if there is a reliance on speculative investments or if there is a lack of regulatory oversight. Financial instability can lead to economic recessions, reduced investment, and loss of wealth.

- **Social Dislocation:**

  Economic development can sometimes result in social dislocation, particularly if there is a shift from rural to urban areas or if traditional communities are disrupted. This can weaken social ties, increase social isolation, and reduce social cohesion.

- **Cultural Erosion:**

  Economic development can sometimes result in cultural erosion, particularly if there is a focus on modernization and globalization. This can lead to a loss of cultural identity, traditions, and values.

Strategies to Address Economic Issues

- **Inclusive Growth:**

  Promote inclusive growth by ensuring that the benefits of economic development are distributed equitably among different social and economic groups.

- **Education and Training:**

  Provide education and training to improve the skills of the workforce and reduce unemployment.

- **Fiscal Responsibility:**

  Practice fiscal responsibility by managing debt levels, maintaining budgetary discipline, and investing in productive assets.

- **Trade Diversification:**

  Diversify trade by expanding into new markets and reducing reliance on a single commodity or market.

- **Resource Management:**

  Implement resource management practices to conserve natural resources and promote sustainable development.

- **Environmental Protection:**

  Implement environmental protection measures to reduce pollution, conserve biodiversity, and mitigate climate change.

- **Financial Regulation:**

  Implement financial regulation to reduce speculation, increase transparency, and promote financial stability.

- **Social Support:**

  Provide social support to communities affected by

economic development, including social services, community engagement, and cultural preservation.

- **Regional Development:**

  Promote regional development to reduce disparities between urban and rural areas and promote balanced growth.

- **International Cooperation:**

  Engage in international cooperation to address global economic issues, including trade imbalances, debt, and environmental degradation.

Economic development can bring many benefits, but it can also lead to economic issues and problems, particularly if the development is not well-planned, inclusive, or sustainable. Addressing these economic issues requires a comprehensive approach, including inclusive growth, education and training, fiscal responsibility, trade diversification, resource management, environmental protection, financial regulation, social support, regional development, and international cooperation. By adopting these strategies, it is possible to achieve economic development that is sustainable, equitable, and beneficial for all.

Political Issues Arising from Economic Advancements

Economic advancements can sometimes lead to political issues and problems, particularly if the benefits of growth are not distributed equitably or if the development process disrupts existing social and political structures. Here are some political issues that can arise due to economic advancements:

- **Political Instability:**

Economic advancements can sometimes lead to political instability, particularly if there is a perception that the benefits of growth are not being distributed fairly. This can lead to social unrest, protests, and even regime changes.

- **Corruption:**

  Economic advancements can sometimes lead to increased corruption, particularly if there is a lack of transparency and accountability in the allocation of resources. Corruption can undermine trust in institutions, reduce the effectiveness of policies, and divert resources away from productive uses.

- **Social Inequality:**

  Economic advancements can sometimes exacerbate social inequalities, particularly if the benefits of growth are concentrated among a small elite. This can lead to social tensions, reduce social mobility, and undermine social cohesion.

- **Policy Capture:**

  Economic advancements can sometimes result in policy capture, where powerful interest groups influence policy decisions to their advantage. This can undermine the public interest, reduce policy effectiveness, and create a sense of disillusionment among citizens.

- **Resource Conflicts:**

  Economic advancements can sometimes lead to resource conflicts, particularly if there is competition for scarce resources, such as land, water, and minerals. Resource conflicts can lead to violence, displacement, and political tensions.

- **Nationalism:**

Economic advancements can sometimes lead to increased nationalism, particularly if there is a perception that external forces are benefiting from the growth. Nationalism can lead to protectionism, xenophobia, and reduced international cooperation.

- **Populism:**

  Economic advancements can sometimes lead to increased populism, particularly if there is a perception that the political establishment is not responsive to the needs of the people. Populism can lead to polarized politics, reduced policy effectiveness, and increased political uncertainty.

- **Environmental Conflicts:**

  Economic advancements can sometimes lead to environmental conflicts, particularly if there is competition for natural resources or if development projects harm the environment. Environmental conflicts can lead to protests, litigation, and political tensions.

- **Regional Disparities:**

  Economic advancements can sometimes lead to regional disparities, particularly if the benefits of growth are concentrated in certain areas. Regional disparities can lead to political tensions, reduce social cohesion, and undermine national unity.

- **Identity Politics:**

  Economic advancements can sometimes lead to increased identity politics, particularly if there is a perception that certain groups are benefiting more than others. Identity politics can lead to polarized politics, reduce social cohesion, and undermine political stability.

Strategies to Address Political Issues

To address these political issues, several strategies can be adopted:

- **Inclusive Growth:**

  Promote inclusive growth by ensuring that the benefits of economic advancements are distributed equitably among different social and economic groups.

- **Transparency and Accountability:**

  Enhance transparency and accountability in the allocation of resources, policy decisions, and the implementation of development projects.

- **Social Policies:**

  Implement social policies to reduce inequalities, improve social mobility, and promote social cohesion.

- **Political Inclusivity:**

  Encourage political inclusivity by involving diverse stakeholders in decision-making processes and ensuring that policy decisions reflect the public interest.

- **Conflict Resolution:**

  Implement conflict resolution mechanisms to address resource conflicts, environmental conflicts, and other disputes arising from economic advancements.

- **Regional Development:**

  Promote regional development to reduce disparities between regions and encourage balanced growth.

- **International Cooperation:**

  Engage in international cooperation to address global political issues, including nationalism, protectionism, and populism.

- **Civic Engagement:**

  Promote civic engagement by encouraging active participation in the political process and fostering a sense of civic responsibility.

- **Rule of Law:**

  Strengthen the rule of law by ensuring that policies and regulations are implemented consistently and fairly.

- **Education and Awareness:**

  Promote education and awareness about political issues and the importance of political participation, particularly among marginalized and underrepresented groups.

Economic advancements can bring many benefits, but they can also lead to political issues and problems, particularly if the benefits of growth are not distributed equitably or if the development process disrupts existing social and political structures. Addressing these political issues requires a comprehensive approach, including inclusive growth, transparency and accountability, social policies, political inclusivity, conflict resolution, regional development, international cooperation, civic engagement, rule of law, and education and awareness. By adopting these strategies, it is possible to achieve economic advancements that are politically sustainable and beneficial for all.

Media Industry Dynamics in Economic Development

Economic advancements can significantly influence the media industry, leading to both opportunities and challenges. Key media-related issues emerging from economic growth include:

- **Media Concentration:**

  Economic advancements can sometimes lead to increased concentration of media ownership, where a small number of companies or individuals control a large share of the media market. This can reduce the diversity of voices and perspectives in the media, and can limit the availability of independent and unbiased information.

- **Media Bias:**

  Economic advancements can sometimes lead to media bias, where media organizations favor certain viewpoints, political parties, or business interests. This can undermine the credibility of the media, reduce public trust in journalism, and limit the ability of the public to make informed decisions.

- **Commercialization of Media:**

  Economic advancements can sometimes lead to increased commercialization of the media, where media organizations prioritize profit-making over journalism. This can result in sensationalism, the prioritization of entertainment over news, and the erosion of journalistic standards.

- **Digital Divide:**

  Economic disparities influence access to digital technologies, and online media is unequal across different social and economic groups. This can limit the ability of certain groups to access information, participate in the digital economy, and engage in online communities.

- **Misinformation and Disinformation:**

  The rapid spread of false or misleading information challenges policy responses and social cohesion. particularly in the digital media environment. This can undermine public discourse, fuel polarization, and reduce the effectiveness of policy responses.

- **Privacy Concerns:**

  Economic advancements can sometimes lead to privacy concerns, particularly with the rise of digital technologies and data-driven media. This can result in the collection and use of personal data without informed consent, and can raise concerns about surveillance, data security, and data ownership.

- **Censorship and Media Freedom Suppression:**

  Economic advancements can sometimes lead to increased censorship and suppression of media freedom, particularly if powerful interests seek to control the narrative or silence dissenting voices. This can undermine democracy, reduce accountability, and limit the ability of the public to hold power to account.

- **Competition for Attention:**

  Intense competition in digital spaces leads to sensationalism and attention-diverting content, particularly with the proliferation of digital media platforms. This can result in information overload, reduced attention spans, and the prioritization of sensational or clickbait content.

- **Algorithmic Bias:**

  Automated content creation can reinforce biases, where algorithms used by digital media platforms prioritize certain content or users based on biased data or biased design. This can reinforce existing biases, limit the diversity of voices, and exacerbate polarization.

- **Media Literacy Deficits:**

Inadequate media literacy impairs the public's ability to critically evaluate content. If media consumption patterns change rapidly or if there is a lack of education about media consumption. This can limit the ability of the public to critically evaluate media content, identify bias, and recognize misinformation.

Strategies for Addressing Media Challenges

Effective mitigation encompasses:

- **Promoting Media Diversity:**

  Encourage media diversity by supporting independent and alternative media outlets, and by promoting pluralism and diversity of voices in the media.

- **Strengthening Regulation:**

  Strengthen media regulation by implementing rules that prevent media concentration, ensure transparency of media ownership, and promote fair and balanced journalism.

- **Enhancing Media Literacy:**

  Enhance media literacy by promoting education and awareness about media consumption, critical thinking, and digital skills.

- **Combating Misinformation:**

  Combat misinformation and disinformation by promoting fact-checking, providing accurate information, and holding those who spread false information accountable.

- **Protecting Media Freedom:**

  Protect media freedom by ensuring that journalists can

work without fear of censorship, intimidation, or violence, and by promoting the right to freedom of expression.

- **Addressing Privacy:**

  Address privacy concerns by implementing data protection laws, ensuring informed consent for data collection and use, and promoting data security and data ownership.

- **Reducing Algorithmic Bias:**

  Reduce algorithmic bias by promoting transparency and accountability in algorithmic design, and by ensuring that algorithms are fair and inclusive.

- **Promoting Digital Inclusion:**

  Support digital inclusion by promoting access to digital technologies and online media for all social and economic groups, and by reducing the digital divide.

- **Encouraging Responsible Advertising:**

  Promote responsible advertising by ensuring that advertising is transparent, ethical, and does not exploit vulnerable groups.

- **Supporting Public Service Media:**

  Foster public service media by supporting media organizations that prioritize journalism, public interest, and social responsibility.

Addressing media industry challenges amid economic growth is vital for sustaining democratic discourse, informed citizenry, and social cohesion. A comprehensive, collaborative approach can enable the media to contribute positively to economic and social development.

Adverse Effects of Economic Advancements on Individuals, Families, and Personal Matters

Economic advancements, while offering numerous benefits, can sometimes lead to challenges and problems at the individual, personal, and family levels. These can manifest in various forms, including behavioral disorders, breakdown of interpersonal relationships, stress, and other complex issues. Here are some of the adverse effects of economic advancements on individuals, families, and personal matters, along with potential interventions to address them:

- **Mental Health Problems:**

  Rapid economic advancement can lead to increased stress, anxiety, depression, and other mental health issues among individuals. Interventions can include promoting work-life balance, providing access to mental health support services, and fostering a culture of empathy and understanding.

- **Family Breakdown:**

  Economic advancements may drive individuals to prioritize career or financial success over family life, leading to strained relationships, divorce, or family breakdown. Interventions can include promoting family values, encouraging quality family time, and providing access to family counseling services.

- **Lifestyle Diseases:**

  Economic advancements can result in sedentary lifestyles, unhealthy eating habits, and increased consumption of processed and junk food, leading to lifestyle diseases like obesity, diabetes, and heart disease. Interventions can include promoting physical activity, encouraging healthy eating habits, and raising awareness about the importance of preventive healthcare.

- **Social Isolation:**

Rapid economic advancements can lead to social isolation as individuals become more focused on their own interests and less connected with others. Interventions can include promoting social interaction, community engagement, and fostering a sense of belonging and connection.

- **Substance Abuse:**

  Economic advancements can sometimes lead to increased substance abuse, as individuals may use drugs or alcohol to cope with stress or enjoy newfound wealth. Interventions can include raising awareness about the dangers of substance abuse, providing access to addiction treatment services, and fostering a supportive environment for recovery.

- **Financial Mismanagement:**

  Rapid economic advancements can lead to financial mismanagement as individuals may struggle to manage their newfound wealth, leading to debt, bankruptcy, or financial instability. Interventions can include promoting financial literacy, providing access to financial planning services, and encouraging responsible spending and saving habits.

- **Disintegration of Traditional Values:**

  Economic advancements can sometimes lead to a disintegration of traditional values, customs, and cultures, as individuals may prioritize modernity and economic success over tradition. Interventions can include promoting cultural preservation, encouraging inter-generational dialogue, and fostering a sense of cultural identity and heritage.

- **Erosion of Work Ethics:**

Economic advancements can sometimes lead to an erosion of work ethics, as individuals may prioritize personal gains over ethical behavior. Interventions can include promoting ethical conduct, providing ethics training, and fostering a culture of integrity and accountability.

- **Personal Identity Crisis:**

  Rapid economic advancements can lead to a personal identity crisis, as individuals may struggle to reconcile their new economic status with their previous identity. Interventions can include providing access to identity formation support, promoting self-reflection, and encouraging individuals to embrace change while staying true to themselves.

- **Interpersonal Conflicts:**

  Economic advancements can sometimes lead to interpersonal conflicts, as individuals may compete for resources, status, or recognition. Interventions can include promoting conflict resolution skills, encouraging open communication, and fostering a culture of respect and understanding.

Economic advancements can bring numerous benefits, but they can also lead to challenges and problems at the individual, personal, and family levels. Addressing these adverse effects requires a comprehensive approach, including promoting mental health, encouraging work-life balance, fostering family values, promoting physical activity, encouraging healthy eating habits, raising awareness about substance abuse, promoting financial literacy, preserving cultural values, promoting ethical conduct, providing identity formation support, and encouraging conflict resolution skills. By adopting these interventions, it is possible to achieve economic advancements that are beneficial for individuals, families, and society at large.

The Impact of Individual Priorities and Short-termism in Economic Advancement

Economic advancements can lead to changes in individual priorities, which can sometimes come at the expense of broader economic well-being. Here are some of the ways in which individual priorities, influenced by economic advancements, can impact economic well-being:

- **Short-Term Focus:**

  Economic advancements can sometimes incentivize individuals to prioritize short-term gains over long-term stability, leading to decisions that may harm long-term economic well-being. For example, individuals may choose to spend rather than save or invest, which can have adverse consequences for future economic stability.

- **Materialism:**

  Rapid economic advancements can lead to increased materialism, with individuals prioritizing material possessions over other aspects of well-being. This can result in excessive consumption, debt, and reduced overall well-being, as individuals may neglect non-material aspects of life such as relationships, health, and community involvement.

- **Income Inequality:**

  Economic advancements can sometimes exacerbate income inequality, as high-income individuals may benefit disproportionately from economic growth. This can lead to social tensions, reduced social mobility, and hindered economic development, as income disparities can result in unequal access to resources and opportunities.

- **Environmental Neglect:**

  Economic advancements can lead to increased consumption and production, which may come at the expense of environmental sustainability. Individuals may prioritize immediate economic gains over long-term environmental well-being, leading to pollution, resource depletion, and climate change, which can ultimately harm economic well-being.

- **Work-Life Imbalance:**

  Economic advancements can sometimes incentivize individuals to prioritize work over other aspects of life, leading to work-life imbalance, burnout, and reduced overall well-being. This can result in decreased productivity and economic growth, as unhealthy and unhappy individuals may contribute less to the economy.

- **Lack of Community Involvement:**

  Economic advancements can lead to increased individualism, with individuals prioritizing their own interests over community well-being. This can result in reduced social cohesion, community engagement, and overall well-being, which can ultimately impact economic stability and growth.

- **Loss of Traditional Values:**

  Economic advancements can sometimes lead to a loss of traditional values, customs, and cultures, as individuals may prioritize modernity and economic success over tradition. This can result in social tensions and reduced overall well-being, as individuals may struggle to reconcile their new economic status with their previous identity.

- **Unethical Behavior:**

  Economic advancements can sometimes incentivize individuals to prioritize personal gains over ethical behavior, leading to unethical decisions that may harm economic well-being. For example, individuals may engage in corruption, fraud, or other unethical practices, which can hinder economic development and reduce overall well-being.

While economic advancements can bring numerous benefits, they can also lead to changes in individual priorities that may come at the expense of broader economic well-being. Addressing these adverse effects requires a comprehensive approach that promotes long-term stability, non-material well-being, income equality, environmental sustainability, work-life balance, community involvement, cultural preservation, and ethical behavior. By adopting these approaches, it is possible to achieve economic advancements that are beneficial for individuals and society at large.

These issues are all significant concerns for economists in today's world. Each of them can have a direct or indirect impact on economic growth and development. Despite the challenges they present, economists are attempting to address them through discussions, dialogues, seminars, conferences, and the formulation of detailed development plans. However, there is a tendency among economists to focus only on their specific area of expertise, often underestimating the broader implications of these issues. Consequently, there is a risk of overlooking important factors or assuming that the problems can be easily resolved.

Economists often believe that many of these issues pertain to specific fields of study and are not directly related to economics. As a result, these problems are sometimes passed from one discipline to another without being adequately addressed, and they persist and worsen over time. Policymakers and economists might respond quickly to these issues in the short-term, but their efforts often fail to mitigate the long-term impact.

The discrepancy between short-term solutions and long-term impacts is a common challenge in policy making and economics. While it's essential to address immediate problems, it is equally crucial to consider the long-term effects of policies and interventions. Here are some reasons why short-term responses might not mitigate long-term impacts:

- **Short-Term Focus:**

  Policymakers and economists might prioritize immediate relief and political gains over long-term solutions. This short-term focus could lead to policies that provide temporary relief but don't address the root causes of the problem.

- **Unintended Consequences:**

  Short-term policies might have unintended negative consequences over time. For example, subsidies or bailouts might provide immediate relief to struggling sectors but could lead to moral hazard, market distortions, or dependency on government support in the long term.

- **Complexity of Economic Systems:**

  Economic systems are complex, and policies can have ripple effects across different sectors and time frames. It's challenging to predict all the long-term consequences of short-term interventions, especially in interconnected global economies.

- **Political Cycles:**

Political cycles often focus on short-term goals due to electoral pressures. Policymakers may prioritize immediate actions that appeal to voters instead of long-term solutions that might not yield visible results within an election cycle.

- **Lack of Comprehensive Approaches:**

  Some issues require comprehensive, multi-faceted approaches involving various stakeholders, including government, private sector, civil society, and international organizations. Short-term responses might not coordinate these stakeholders effectively or address the complexity of the problem.

- **Resource Constraints:**

  Policymakers and economists might face budgetary, personnel, or other resource constraints that limit their ability to implement long-term solutions. Short-term responses might be more feasible within these constraints but may not be sufficient to address long-term impacts.

- **Uncertainty:**

  The future is uncertain, and it's challenging to predict all potential long-term impacts accurately. Policymakers and economists might focus on addressing known immediate issues rather than attempting to mitigate uncertain future impacts.

If the aforementioned problems and issues are not taken into account before proposing or implementing economic laws, assumptions, theories, and empirical studies, the efforts are likely to be in vain. They may yield no positive effects or only short-term results without offering a permanent solution, leading to incomplete economic development. In my view, this is akin to putting money into a bag with holes; the hard work and efforts of economists may not bear fruit, and their theories and laws have a lower chance of success.

Addressing potential problems and issues before proposing or implementing economic laws, assumptions, theories, and empirical studies is crucial to ensure the effectiveness and validity of these efforts. Failing to do so can lead to inaccurate or incomplete results and may even have negative consequences for economies and societies. Here are a few reasons why considering potential problems and issues is essential:

- **Unintended Consequences:**

  Economic policies and theories can have unintended consequences that may not be immediately apparent. Without thorough consideration of potential negative outcomes, policies could end up exacerbating existing issues or creating new problems.

- **Incomplete Analysis:**

  Ignoring potential problems can lead to incomplete analysis, making it difficult to predict how different factors may interact or influence outcomes. This can result in inaccurate conclusions and recommendations.

- **Bias and Assumptions:**

  Economic theories and models are often built on assumptions that might not hold true in all circumstances. Failing to challenge these assumptions can result in biased results that don't accurately reflect real-world situations.

- **Ethical and Social Implications:**

  Economic decisions can have ethical and social implications. Ignoring these aspects can lead to policies that are not in line with societal values, causing public backlash and social unrest.

- **Data Quality and Availability:**

Economic studies heavily rely on data. Neglecting data quality and availability issues can lead to inaccurate or unreliable results, undermining the credibility of the research.

- **Complex Interactions:**

  Economic systems are complex and interconnected. Failing to consider potential interactions between different economic variables can lead to oversimplified conclusions that don't capture the full picture.

- **Changing Circumstances:**

  Economic conditions and circumstances can change rapidly. Policies and theories that do not take these changes into account can quickly become obsolete or ineffective.

To address these concerns, economists and policymakers often engage in rigorous analysis, model testing, scenario simulations, and peer review. They also draw on historical examples and empirical evidence to gain a better understanding of potential issues and challenges. Furthermore, interdisciplinary collaboration can provide valuable insights by incorporating perspectives from fields like sociology, psychology, and political science to better understand the real-world implications of economic decisions.

In summary, considering potential problems and issues before proposing or implementing economic laws, assumptions, theories, and empirical studies is a vital step to ensure the relevance, accuracy, and positive impact of economic research and policy-making efforts.

The Limits of Methodology and the Importance of Root Cause Analysis in Economics

In the realm of current economic research, a consensus emerges from a diverse array of methods and methodologies. However, the incorporation of new techniques remains confined within a limited circle. This narrowing of focus inevitably amplifies the dimensions and intricacies of the challenges at hand. To illustrate, envision a patient seeking medical attention for a severe, chronic ailment. When attended to by a proficient and skilled physician, the root of the issue is accurately pinpointed, leading to precise diagnoses and efficient recovery strategies. Conversely, if the physician lacks expertise, there's a tendency to prolong the diagnostic process, potentially exacerbating the condition. Consequently, misguided treatment approaches could inadvertently convolute the patient's state, emphasizing the significance of accurate medical guidance. Similarly, in economics, embracing diverse methodologies akin to the proficient doctor can prevent undue complexities and uncertainties from infiltrating the problems being addressed.

Similarly, the present-day economy grapples with a multitude of persistent ailments. Regrettably, without exhaustive scrutiny, economists are hastily prescribing a handful of remedies, neglecting the imperative of delving into the fundamental underpinnings of these issues. Had they managed to successfully unearth the "root cause," the need to navigate through such crises and numerous other economic predicaments might have been obviated.

Consequently, economists find themselves in a state of perplexity, contending with diverse schools of thought, a multitude of economic policy perspectives, and a range of considered methodologies to address prevailing issues. Despite their earnest efforts, the complexity of these challenges keeps economists engrossed in the absence of definitive solutions. Typically, economists are expected to unravel societal and governmental quandaries, yet the current circumstances have proven exceptionally demanding.

However, it's also clear that the aforementioned circumstances have been brought about by economists who have evaluated the "worth of labor" solely through the lens of its monetary value. This perspective has equated the "dignity of labor" with its potential for enhancing economic growth and profitability, leading to a measurement based on "wealth/money" within societies or for humanity as a whole.

Rather than placing significant emphasis on the welfare and structure of society, economists have predominantly directed their attention towards profit generation and maximizing gains from every avenue. This shift in focus has resulted in a narrowing or diminishing of their role, reputation, and credibility within both society and the state. An economist's primary allegiance should be to the betterment of society and its organizational framework. Disregarding this pivotal aspect and fixating on other matters could potentially lead astray, jeopardizing economic progress and advancement.

The cornerstone of economics lies in its central focus on the consumer or economic agent, with its foundations rooted in the intricacies of consumer behavior, individual inclinations, and preferences. A profound interconnection exists, along with a cause-and-effect dynamic, between the conduct of each economic entity and the advancement of the economy.

Thus, the prevailing market-oriented framework and its operations have evolved by meticulously considering the feedback of consumers (economic agents). This process involves proactive measures and thorough research to create a diverse range of consumer goods and services, as well as to comprehend the dynamics of supply and demand, pricing mechanisms, and the streamlined dissemination of pertinent information. Market participants leverage this insight to craft increasingly appealing products and services tailored to the preferences of economic agents. However, economists erred in judgment by disregarding these crucial considerations, thereby steering society and the state down a course that has failed to address the challenges currently confronting us. The situation has grown more intricate, underscoring the fact that we find ourselves ensnared in a cycle of a "vicious circle," akin to navigating treacherous terrain or descending into the depths of an economic quagmire.

The Vicious Circle: A Metaphor for Modern Economic Challenges

The evolving complexity of the situation highlights the reality that we are now caught in a self-perpetuating cycle, often referred to as a "vicious circle." This analogy draws parallels to traversing hazardous landscapes or sinking deeper into an economic crisis. In this context, a "vicious circle" typically implies a situation where multiple negative factors reinforce each other, leading to a worsening state. Each negative factor exacerbates the others, creating a self-reinforcing loop that can be challenging to break free from. The mention of "navigating treacherous terrain" underscores the difficulty and uncertainty of the situation, while the reference to "descending into the depths of an economic quagmire" suggests a complex and potentially inescapable economic downturn.

Overall, the imagery used paints a picture of a challenging and intricate situation that is progressively becoming more difficult to navigate or resolve. The term "vicious circle" encapsulates the idea that the negative factors are feeding off each other, making it harder to find a way out.

The comparison to "navigating treacherous terrain" and "descending into the depths of an economic quagmire" adds depth to the understanding of the situation's complexity and difficulty. Let's break down the imagery further:

- **Navigating Treacherous Terrain:**

This comparison conjures an image of a hazardous landscape where the path ahead is uncertain and fraught with challenges. Just as one must tread carefully and make calculated decisions when navigating through treacherous terrain, the situation being described requires careful consideration and strategic thinking to avoid pitfalls and make progress.

- **Descending into the Depths of an Economic Quagmire:**

  Here, the imagery points to an economic scenario that is sinking into a quagmire, a difficult and mucky situation that is tough to extricate oneself from. A quagmire suggests a complex and sticky predicament, much like an economic crisis that gets progressively worse due to the interplay of various negative factors.

Both comparisons emphasize the intricate and precarious nature of the situation. They evoke a sense of urgency, implying that decisive and well-informed actions are necessary to avoid further complications or to climb out of the challenging circumstances. The language used in these comparisons heightens the emotional impact of the description and underscores the seriousness of the situation at hand. To break free from the grip of the vicious circle and attain success in extricating ourselves, it is imperative that we delve into the "root cause." Neglecting this critical step could exacerbate the complexities we face, rendering the search for an effective resolution an insurmountable challenge. Hence, vigilance across all fronts is essential.

CHAPTER 9

Institution-Building and Public Buy-in

Economists need to grasp the philosophy and structure of society in order to provide solutions to complex economic problems. Economic problems do not occur in isolation—they are embedded within the social, cultural, and political fabric of a society. Understanding these contexts allows economists to offer more relevant and effective solutions.

Without strong institutions and genuine public buy-in, even the best-designed policies fail. This chapter provides frameworks for institutional development, stakeholder engagement, and building the social contract necessary for transformative change.

The Centrality of Institutions in Development

What Are Institutions and Why Do They Matter?

Definition:

Institutions are the "rules of the game" in society the formal laws, regulations, and informal norms that shape human interaction, constrain behavior, and create incentives. They include:

Formal Institutions:

- Constitutional frameworks
- Legal systems (property rights, contracts, dispute resolution)
- Regulatory bodies (central bank, securities regulator, competition commission)
- Government bureaucracy (civil service, public agencies)
- Electoral systems and political structures

Informal Institutions:

- Social norms and customs
- Trust networks and reciprocity
- Cultural values and beliefs
- Unwritten codes of conduct
- Community enforcement mechanisms

Why Institutions Matter for Development:

1. **Reduce Transaction Costs:**

    1. Clear property rights lower costs of exchange
    2. Contract enforcement makes trade possible

3. Predictable regulations reduce business uncertainty

2. **Shape Incentives:**

   1. Meritocratic civil service → better governance
   2. Independent judiciary → investor confidence
   3. Transparent procurement → reduced corruption

3. **Enable Coordination:**

   1. Central bank coordinates monetary policy
   2. Standards bodies enable interoperability
   3. Electoral systems aggregate preferences

4. **Build Trust:**

   1. Consistent rule application → predictability
   2. Checks and balances → accountability
   3. Public participation → legitimacy

5. **Accumulate Knowledge:**

   1. Bureaucratic memory preserves expertise
   2. Research institutions generate evidence
   3. Educational institutions transmit knowledge across generations

9.1. Institutional Quality and Economic Outcomes

Empirical Evidence:

Cross-country studies consistently show strong correlations between institutional quality and development outcomes:

Table 9.1: Institutional Quality and Economic Performanc

Institutional Quality Quartile	GDP per Capita (PPP $)	GDP Growth (% annual)	FDI (% of GDP)	Corruption Perception Index
Q1 (Weakest institutions)	8,450	2.8%	1.2%	28
Q2	18,200	4.1%	2.3%	42
Q3	32,500	4.8%	3.8%	56
Q4 (Strongest institutions)	58,900	3.2%	4.5%	72

Note: Data from 180 countries, World Bank Governance Indicators 2023. Q4 has higher GDP but slower growth (convergence effect).

Regression Analysis:

log(GDP_per_capita) = $\alpha + \beta \times$ Institutional_Quality_Index + controls

$\beta = 0.82$ (SE = 0.11, $p<0.001$)

$R^2 = 0.68$

Interpretation: 1-point improvement in institutional quality index (0-100 scale) → 0.82% higher GDP per capita

For India (Institutional Quality Index = 54):

1. If improved to 70 (Malaysia level): +13.1% GDP per capita = ₹41,500 additional per person
2. Aggregate gain: ₹57.5 lakh crore

India's Institutional Landscape

Strengths:

- Democratic continuity (75+ years)
- Independent judiciary and election commission
- Vibrant civil society and free press
- Federal structure enabling policy experimentation
- Strong scientific and technical institutions (IITs, ISRO, etc.)

Weaknesses:

- **Bureaucratic delays:** Average project clearance time: 18 months
- **Judicial backlog:** 4.4 crore pending cases, average disposal time: 5-7 years
- **Corruption:** Ranks 93rd out of 180 countries (CPI 2023)
- **Capacity gaps:** 25% vacancies in civil service, 40% in judiciary
- **Fragmentation:** Overlapping mandates, coordination failures across agencies
- **Political interference:** Erosion of autonomy in regulatory bodies

Institutional Quality Score:

Dimension	Score (0-100)	Global Percentile
Voice & Accountability	58.3	62nd
Political Stability	42.1	48th
Government Effectiveness	54.8	56th
Regulatory Quality	52.3	54th
Rule of Law	51.9	53rd
Control of Corruption	47.2	49th
Overall Average	51.1	52nd percentile

Source: World Bank Worldwide Governance Indicators 2023

India ranks in the middle globally, significant room for improvement.

9.2 Understanding the Family as the Core Economic Unit

Proposition and Strategic Framework for Economic Expansion

My proposition and strategy for fostering economic expansion and progress begins with a foundational assertion: every economic activity and behavior stems from the "family" unit. If economists analyze individuals isolated from their familial context, this detachment can exacerbate the issues previously outlined. This occurs because individuals, or economic agents, inherently depend on their families as the fundamental societal units.

The array of challenges (enumerated as A through I) fundamentally trace back to a single root cause the erosion of the "family structure" within our society. The rapid transformation of family dynamics has led to a precarious economic environment, akin to navigating quicksand. It is imperative to recognize that every human decision-making process is deeply entwined with the concept of family.

This interconnectedness rests upon individual conduct, attitudes, preferences, needs, wants, and actions .

The significance of family in shaping economic behavior cannot be overstated. The interrelation between familial bonds and economic choices is profound, influencing not only individual well-being but also broader societal and economic outcomes.

The central question revolves around how individuals maintain moral and ethical consistency. The solution lies in redefining, restructuring, and rejuvenating the family structure in harmony with its ongoing evolution .

The Significance of Family in Shaping Economic Behavior

The significance of family in shaping economic behavior cannot be overstated. The interrelation between familial bonds and economic choices is profound, influencing not only individual well-being but also broader societal and economic outcomes.

Economic Functions of Families:

1. **Resource Pooling and Risk-Sharing:**
    - Families share income across members (employed → unemployed/elderly/children)
    - Smooth consumption during shocks (illness, job loss)
    - Informal insurance mechanism (stronger than markets in many contexts)

2. **Human Capital Formation:**

    - Parents invest in children's education, health, nutrition
    - Intergenerational transmission of skills, knowledge, values
    - Early childhood environment shapes lifetime outcomes

3. **Social Capital Creation:**

    - Families instill trust, reciprocity, civic duty
    - Teach cooperation, conflict resolution
    - Connect individuals to broader social networks

4. **Labor Supply Decisions:**

    - Household members coordinate work, caregiving
    - Women's labor force participation linked to family support systems
    - Migration decisions often family-based (send remittances)

5. **Savings and Investment:**

    - Families save for children's education, weddings, old age
    - Investment decisions reflect family goals (home, business)
    - Bequest motives shape accumulation

6. **Consumption Patterns:**

    - Household-level consumption smoothing
    - Scale economies (public goods within family)
    - Preferences shaped by family culture

Evidence of Family's Role in Economic Outcomes

Intergenerational Mobility:

Children's outcomes strongly predict by parents' status (Chapter 6, Table 6.4):

- 42.7% of children born in bottom income quintile remain there (vs. 20% if perfect mobility)

- Family background explains ~60% of variation in earnings (intergenerational elasticity = 0.58)

Family Structure and Child Outcomes:

Family Structure	Avg Years of Schooling	Test Scores (SD)	Health (0-100)	Future Earnings (₹ lakh/ year)
Two-parent, stable	11.2	0.15	78.5	4.8
Two-parent, unstable (divorce, conflict)	9.8	-0.22	72.3	3.9
Single-parent	8.5	-0.38	68.2	3.2
Extended family (grandparents, etc.)	10.1	-0.05	75.8	4.3

Note: Controlling for income, education of parents. Test scores standardized. Data from longitudinal surveys.

Finding: Stable two-parent families produce best outcomes, but extended families also provide strong support. Single parenthood associated with disadvantages (though causality complex such as poverty, stress may drive both single parenthood and poor outcomes).

9.3 Strategic Approaches to Family Structure Evolution

Recognizing that family structures evolve alongside social, cultural, and technological shifts, the following strategies offer pathways for revitalization:

- **Redefining:** Adapt to emerging family forms, including single-parent, blended, and multi-generational households, to embrace inclusivity.
- **Restructuring:** Reassess and reshape family roles to reflect flexibility, collaboration, and individual strengths.
- **Rejuvenating:** Prioritize bonding activities, revisit cherished traditions, and cultivate new rituals aligning with contemporary family dynamics.
- **Reshaping:** Embrace open communication and mutual respect to facilitate adaptation to change and novel perspectives.
- **Remodeling:** Modify traditional structures collaboratively to foster harmonious and welcoming family environments.
- **Reevaluation:** Periodically assess family health and dynamics, seeking professional support as needed.
- **Renewal:** Celebrate familial bonds through shared experiences, empathy, and reinforced connections.

Successfully implementing these measures encourages resilient, adaptive family units equipped to thrive amid modern complexities. The intrinsic connection between family and economic behavior reflects deep social and cultural embedded; family dynamics significantly influence individual decisions and societal structures. Redefinition and restructuring initiatives must consider the dynamism of family evolution to effectively sustain economic and social stability.

The current state of the family structure is so degraded that we cannot simply cure or restore it to its previous state. Analogous to medical practice, where a patient who does not respond to traditional treatment may require surgery to regain health, we must make radical decisions akin to "surgical interventions in the economy of the family" to rehabilitate our family society.

Applying Surgical Principles to Family Economic framework:

- **Identify the Problem:**

  Just as surgery begins with an accurate diagnosis, families must assess their financial situations, identify sources of stress, and understand root economic challenges.

- **Evaluate Your Options:**

  Surgery is often a last resort after other treatments fail. Similarly, prior to significant changes in family economics, all alternative methods to increase income, reduce expenses, or manage debt should be considered.

- **Seek Expert Advice:**

  Families should consult with financial experts, just as patients seek specialized surgeons. This could include financial planners, tax professionals, or trusted advisors with the relevant expertise.

- **Weigh Risks and Benefits:**

  Like surgery, financial decisions carry risks and potential benefits. Careful evaluation aligned with long-term family goals and values is essential.

- **Make a Plan and Execute:**

  After selecting the best course, detailed planning and execution such as budgeting, debt management, or investment adjustment are required.

- **Monitor and Adjust:**

  Continuous financial monitoring and adjustment, akin to post-surgical follow-ups, are critical to staying on track.

- **Communication:**

  Open and honest family communication about decisions, rationales, and responsibilities fosters collective accountability.

This systematic approach enables families to restore and rejuvenate their economic framework, setting the stage for long-term success. The maxim "prevention is better than cure" reminds us to address these issues urgently to avoid being trapped in a vicious cycle difficult to break. Despite this imperative, consensus on comprehensive solutions remains elusive. Most experts propose alternative or partial measures but rarely recommend a "comprehensive solution"

A comprehensive solution requires a holistic approach and is often hard to define due to the unique circumstances of each family and the diverse range of factors involved in their economic framework. However, a comprehensive solution is possible by combining multiple strategies and customizing them to fit the family's specific needs.

Steps to Create a Comprehensive Solution

- **Engage in an In-Depth Analysis**

  Work with a financial planner or trusted expert to conduct a thorough analysis of income, expenses, debts, savings, investments, and other financial assets or liabilities. Identify patterns over time and opportunities for improvement.

- **Address Immediate Concerns**

  Prioritize urgent financial issues such as high-interest debt or the absence of emergency savings. Temporary sacrifices or resource reallocation may be necessary.

- **Create a Long-Term Financial Plan**

  Develop a plan aligned with family goals including strategies for saving, investing, debt management, and expense reduction. Incorporate major life events such as home buying, education, and retirement.

- **Implement Behavior Changes**

  Tackle behaviors contributing to financial difficulties (e.g., overspending) with strategies like automated savings, budgeting tools, and accountability support from family members.

- **Build a Support Network**

  Involve all family members in financial discussions and decision-making. Promote financial literacy and responsible money management collectively.

- **Review and Revise Regularly**

  Periodically evaluate the plan and adjust based on changing income, expenses, or life circumstances. Continuous monitoring ensures long-term success.

By integrating these elements, families can forge solutions that address immediate pressures while setting the foundation for enduring financial stability. Only by reforming families and society at large can we protect our economic, environmental, and social well-being. Even as innovations advance in high-speed computing, satellite technology, robotics, and policy making, without ethical guidance and social sensitivity, these will ultimately falter.

9.4 Challenges of Technological Advances

- **Unequal Access:**

  Advanced technologies can widen social and economic inequalities if access is uneven, granting disproportionate advantages to some.

- **Job Displacement:**

  Automation may displace workers, especially in labor-intensive industries. Adequate workforce training and support are essential.

- **Privacy Concerns:**

  The proliferation of data collection raises alarming privacy issues. Ethical regulation is critical to prevent misuse.

- **Environmental Impact:**

  Production and disposal of high-tech equipment contribute to pollution and resource depletion, raising sustainability concerns in a rapidly evolving tech landscape.

- **Policy Shortcomings:**

  Poorly crafted or shortsighted policies can generate unintended negative social, economic, and environmental consequences.

- **Ethical Dilemmas:**

  Emerging technologies, including AI and biotechnology, challenge our understanding of rights, identity, and societal values. Inclusive and careful deliberation is necessary.

Strategies to Mitigate Adverse Effects of Technology

- Ensure equitable access to technology, education, and opportunities.
- Provide workforce training and support for displaced workers.
- Implement comprehensive regulations and ethical guidelines governing technology.
- Promote sustainable manufacturing and technology disposal methods.
- Engage diverse stakeholders in policy making.
- Foster transparent dialogue around ethical challenges and societal impact.

By addressing these complex challenges in an integrated, ethical, and inclusive manner, technological advancements can propel society toward greater equity, sustainability, and justice, reinforcing the foundational role of families and communities.

CHAPTER 10

AI, Disruption, and the Modernized World

Contemporary economic narratives often promote the idea of double work for women under the banners of empowerment, freedom, and inclusion. While these objectives are important, such frameworks frequently overlook a critical reality: a vast range of women's contributions remains economically invisible and structurally unaccounted for.

Activities such as nurturing values, making personal sacrifices, building and sustaining households, transmitting culture, and shaping future generations are foundational to societal stability and long-term economic resilience. Yet, in predominantly materialistic and market-centric economic models, these contributions are either excluded from formal valuation or treated as non-productive, leading to a systematic undervaluation of women's real economic and social capital.

This omission does not represent empowerment; rather, it reflects a misalignment in how economies define productivity and value.

By failing to recognize and integrate these contributions into economic thinking and policy, societies underutilize women's full capacities—not only as participants in markets, but as architects of culture, continuity, and sustainable development across generations.

A truly progressive and sustainable economic framework must move beyond narrow output-based metrics and incorporate the full spectrum of women's contributions—both visible and invisible— into its models, measurements, and policy decisions. Progress and innovation in technology and policy-making are essential, but alone, they cannot resolve the broader challenges confronting our societies, families, and environment. Effective reform requires a comprehensive vision that acknowledges the deep interconnections across social, economic, and ecological domains.

10.1 Automation & Labor Market Disruption

Table 10.1: Job Automation Risk by Sector (India)

Sector	Employment (millions)	Employment (millions)	Jobs at Risk (millions)	Timeline	Mitigation Strategy
Manufacturing	58	67%	38.9	5-10 years	Reskilling in maintenance, programming
Retail & Wholesale	42	52%	21.8	10-15 years	Shift to experiential retail, customer service
Transport & Logistics	28	78%	21.8	5-15 years	Transition to fleet management, last-mile coordination
Agriculture	195	38%	74.1	15-25 years	Precision farming, agritech services

Construction	55	45%	24.8	10-20 years	Project management, specialized trades
IT & Services	18	22%	4.0	Ongoing	Continuous upskilling, AI collaboration
Healthcare	12	15%	1.8	Long-term	Focus on empathy, complex diagnosis
Education	9	18%	1.6	Long-term	Personalized learning, mentorship
Total	417	45%	188.8	Variable	

Note: "High automation risk" = >70% of tasks automatable with current/near-future technology. Timeline = when automation becomes cost-effective at scale.

Interpretation:

- 188.8 million jobs (45% of workforce) at high risk by 2040
- Manufacturing, transport most vulnerable (routine physical tasks)
- Healthcare, education most protected (human touch essential)

10.2 Digital Divide & Inequality

Table 10.2: Digital Access Gaps (India 2023)

Dimension	Urban	Rural	Gap	Bottom Quintile	Top Quintile	Gap
Smartphone ownership (%)	82%	43%	39pp	31%	94%	63pp
Internet access at home (%)	71%	28%	43pp	18%	92%	74pp
Internet access at home (%)	68%	31%	37pp	22%	86%	64pp
Internet access at home (%)	64%	19%	45pp	12%	81%	69pp
Digital payment usage (%)	76%	34%	42pp	25%	88%	63pp

Consequence: Without intervention, automation + digital divide = massive inequality spike

Key Considerations for Achieving Sustainable Reform

1. **Empower Communities:** Empower local communities to take charge of their development, with a focus on education, community engagement, and sustainable resource management. By supporting local initiatives, we can create a more robust and self-reliant community structure that reduces dependence on external resources and fosters a sense of ownership and accountability.
2. **Strengthen Family Systems:** Encourage strong and supportive family systems where members are educated on financial literacy, responsible consumption, and sustainable living. Families can serve as the foundation for teaching values such as empathy, responsibility, and stewardship, which are essential for building a sustainable

society.

3. **Promote Environmental Stewardship:** Advocate for responsible environmental practices and policies at the local, national, and international levels. This includes conservation efforts, pollution reduction, sustainable agriculture, and the promotion of clean energy sources. Environmental stewardship should be incorporated into every aspect of society, from individual choices to corporate practices and government policies.
4. **Cultivate Ethical Leadership:** Foster ethical leadership in government, business, and civic organizations. Leaders who prioritize long-term benefits over short-term gains and consider the impact of their decisions on the broader community and environment can drive systemic change and create a culture of accountability and responsibility.
5. **Collaboration and Multilateralism:** Recognize that the challenges we face are interconnected and require collaboration between nations, sectors, and communities. Encourage multilateral efforts to address global challenges such as climate change, economic inequality, and social injustice.
6. **Invest in Education and Awareness:** Invest in education and awareness campaigns to inform the public about the importance of sustainable practices, the impact of their choices, and the need for collective action. Education is a powerful tool for empowering individuals to make informed decisions and contribute to positive change.

By taking a holistic approach to reform that addresses the interconnectedness of family, society, and the environment, we can create a sustainable and equitable world for current and future generations. Such an approach recognizes that true progress and well-being are measured not only by technological advancements but also by the quality of life, social harmony, and environmental health we achieve.

Even if we were to develop technology capable of handling everything, the growing complexity, compounded by human wisdom, would likely only worsen the situation rather than resolve it. Such a suggestion needs to be considered both accurately and efficiently, and it requires reshaping the family system as soon as possible. If this isn't taken seriously, both we and our future generations will bear the consequences.

Changing human nature to transform individual behavior can be difficult. Even with strong determination, success may be partial or achieved only to a certain extent. This could involve improving physical or mental health through establishing hospitals and engaging psychiatrists, humanists, realists, sociologists, human rights groups, national and international organizations, governments, and other institutions

Observing that changing human nature and transforming individual behavior can be a complex and challenging process. Behavior change is multifaceted and influenced by a variety of factors, including individual psychology, social influences, environmental conditions, and access to resources. It's also an ongoing process that may require sustained effort and support.

Considering this complexity, a collaborative approach involving various stakeholders, such as healthcare professionals, humanists, sociologists, human rights groups, governments, and international organizations, is essential. Here are some strategies for facilitating meaningful behavior change:

1. **Education and Awareness:** Provide information and

education about the benefits of adopting healthier behaviors, the risks associated with unhealthy behaviors, and the importance of taking responsibility for one's health and well-being.

2. **Creating Supportive Environments:** Create environments that support and encourage healthy behaviors. This could include access to healthy food options, safe spaces for physical activity, and resources for mental and emotional well-being.

3. **Personalized Interventions:** Recognize that behavior change is a personal journey, and interventions should be tailored to an individual's unique needs, preferences, and circumstances. Collaborate with healthcare professionals to develop personalized plans and interventions.

4. **Community Engagement:** Engage communities in the process of behavior change. Encourage community- led initiatives, support groups, and local resources that foster a sense of collective responsibility and provide a strong support network for individuals.

5. **Positive Reinforcement:** Use positive reinforcement to encourage healthy behaviors. Recognize and reward efforts to adopt healthier behaviors, celebrate achievements, and provide incentives for continued progress.

6. **Empowerment and Self-efficacy:** Empower individuals to take control of their health and well-being. Help them build confidence, develop coping skills, and increase their self-efficacy to sustain long-term behavior change.

7. **Policy and Advocacy:** Advocate for policies that promote

healthy behaviors and support behavior change efforts. Address systemic barriers, such as socioeconomic disparities and lack of access to resources, that hinder behavior change

8. **Multidisciplinary Approach:** Recognize that behavior change involves physical, mental, emotional, and social factors. Collaborate with a diverse group of professionals, including psychiatrists, sociologists, and human rights advocates, to address these interconnected factors holistically.

9. **Monitoring and Evaluation:** Continuously monitor and evaluate behavior change initiatives to assess their effectiveness and make necessary adjustments. Collect data, measure outcomes, and seek feedback from participants to inform future efforts.

10. **Cultural Sensitivity:** Respect cultural differences and values when designing and implementing behavior change initiatives. Engage with local communities, involve them in decision-making, and ensure that interventions are culturally appropriate and relevant.

By taking a holistic, multidisciplinary, and collaborative approach, we can create an environment that supports and facilitates behavior change, ultimately improving individual and community health and well-being.

These bodies might employ various strategies, including creating comprehensive plans, enacting numerous constitutional provisions and clauses, introducing and innovating countless technological tools and products, fostering thousands of positive ideas and solutions, and defining personal and societal goals and responsibilities in economic, social, and political terms.

10.3 The Human Shield Against Disruption

Character formation typically occurs during childhood, and if not cultivated at this stage, it can become challenging or even impossible to develop later. As we observe today, the root of many issues affecting society, the economy, nature, the environment, health, and systemic dilemmas and crises can be traced back to the breakdown of the family system, the diminishing importance of family relationships, or a complete disregard for the value of relationships.

The foundation of character is established during childhood, and if not formed at this early stage, it becomes difficult or even impossible to change later on. As we can observe today, the root cause of many societal, economic, environmental, health, and systemic dilemmas and crises is the collapse of the family system, the diminishing value of family relationships, or the complete devaluation of relationships altogether.

Nonetheless, it's important to examine how the family system collapsed. What are the primary concerns and causes? Who was responsible for this collapse, and how did it come about? We need to highlight these issues. For instance, some concerns could be listed as follows:

Economists have often placed little emphasis on humanity and human values, instead introducing the concept of the "value of labor." In this theory, women are considered a product and a primary source of labor, with their domestic work being viewed as having no economic value. As a result, women were encouraged or drawn to work outside the home, and priority was given to creating jobs for women to portray them as active economic participants. This approach stems from the misguided belief that all problems can be solved through wealth or money. In reality, this has only made the situation more complex and problematic. An important critique of economic theories that have historically devalued or overlooked the contributions of women, particularly in the realm of domestic work. It's essential to recognize that traditional economic models often reflect a limited and narrow perspective on value and labor. By prioritizing monetary value and formal employment over other forms of work and contributions, these models can perpetuate gender inequities and distort our understanding of what constitutes valuable and meaningful labor.

The concept of the "value of labor" has often been focused on market transactions and formal employment, failing to consider the broader spectrum of labor that includes unpaid domestic work, caregiving, and community contributions. This oversight has had several consequences:

1. **Undervaluing Domestic Work:** Domestic work, which includes tasks such as cooking, cleaning, and caregiving, is often undervalued or considered "invisible" labor because it is typically unpaid and occurs outside the formal economy. Women disproportionately shoulder the burden of domestic work, and their contributions often go unrecognized.
2. **Impact on Women's Economic Opportunities:** The pressure to participate in the formal economy and the simultaneous expectation to fulfill domestic responsibilities can place a double burden on women. This can limit their ability to pursue educational and economic opportunities, advance in their careers, and achieve financial independence.
3. **Reinforcing Gender Stereotypes:** The devaluation of domestic work and the emphasis on formal employment

can reinforce traditional gender roles and stereotypes, hindering progress toward gender equality.

4. **Narrow Definition of Economic Value:** The focus on monetary transactions and formal employment as the primary measures of economic value limits our understanding of the broader contributions that individuals and communities make to society. This narrow definition can lead to policies and practices that prioritize short-term economic gains over long-term societal well-being.
5. **Misguided Approach to Problem Solving:** The belief that wealth or money can solve all problems overlooks the complex and interconnected nature of societal challenges. Economic growth is only one dimension of development, and a more holistic approach is needed to address issues such as gender inequality, social justice, and environmental sustainability.

To address these issues, it's important to adopt a more inclusive and holistic approach to economics that recognizes the value of all forms of labor, including unpaid domestic work, and considers the broader contributions of individuals and communities to societal well-being. This approach should prioritize human values, gender equality, and social justice and move beyond a narrow focus on monetary wealth as the sole measure of value and success.

10.4 The Undervaluation of Women's Contributions in Economic Thought

Economists have historically argued that women's contributions to the economy, particularly as measured by GDP, were minimal or nonexistent. Consequently, women were often seen as non-economic agents whose labor did not add economic value. This perspective led many economists to advocate for increasing women's participation in production and other economic activities outside the home.

However, this viewpoint profoundly undervalued women's multifaceted roles and responsibilities. It also distorted the economic structure by promoting a misguided emphasis on monetary wealth and market activity, thereby sidelining essential social and familial dimensions of economic life .

Indeed, the traditional economic approach has often failed to account for women's full contributions to the economy, particularly their unpaid labor in domestic work and care giving. This narrow view of economic value has led to distorted policies and perceptions that prioritize formal employment and monetary gains over other forms of valuable labor. It is essential to address these shortcomings and recognize the broader spectrum of women's contributions to societal well-being.

The misguided emphasis on monetary wealth as the primary measure of value and success has had several negative consequences:

1. **Inequitable Distribution of Labor:** The devaluation of unpaid domestic work and care giving has led to an unequal distribution of labor, with women often bearing the brunt of these responsibilities. This inequity limits women's ability to participate fully in the formal economy, access educational and economic opportunities, and achieve financial independence.
2. **Misrepresentation of Economic Contributions:** By focusing solely on formal employment and monetary transactions, traditional economic models have misrepresented women's contributions to the economy. This misrepresentation can perpetuate gender inequities

and hinder the development of policies that support women's full participation in economic and societal life.

3. **Reinforcement of Gender Stereotypes:** The emphasis on formal employment as the primary measure of economic value can reinforce traditional gender roles and stereotypes. This narrow view of value can hinder progress toward gender equality and social justice.
4. **Distorted Economic Structure:** The prioritization of formal employment and monetary gains can distort the economic structure, leading to policies and practices that prioritize short-term economic gains over long-term societal well-being. This distorted perspective can contribute to economic inequality, social tensions, and environmental degradation
5. **Materialistic Focus:** The narrow focus on monetary wealth as the sole measure of value and success can contribute to a materialistic culture that prioritizes status, possessions, and wealth over human values, relationships, and community well-being.

To address these challenges, it is essential to adopt a more holistic and inclusive approach to economics that recognizes the full spectrum of women's contributions to societal well-being, including unpaid domestic work and caregiving. This approach should prioritize human values, gender equality, and social justice over a narrow focus on monetary wealth. By broadening our understanding of economic value and recognizing the importance of all forms of labor, we can create a more equitable and sustainable economy that benefits everyone.

Humanists and ideologists have encouraged women to move away from traditional home roles with promises of wealth and independence. However, this shift has only intensified the complexity of societal challenges. Human rights activists and organizations have often granted rights to individuals without insisting on corresponding responsibilities. This oversight fosters a societal divide where individuals expect rights without embracing obligations.

Under the banner of "gender equality," policies have sometimes perpetuated inequality. Instead of deeply valuing women's intrinsic worth, political reservations and job quotas have emphasized superficial attributes, misdirecting focus from authentic capabilities. Fundamental biological and psychological differences between genders present inherent challenges to achieving absolute equality. Women's unique roles such as childbearing and qualities like gentleness, empathy, and resilience, often go unappreciated or are exploited for commercial interests rather than genuine respect.

The consequences of these misguided approaches manifest in compounded societal and national issues, underscoring the urgency of restoring respect for women, especially within familial contexts, and prioritizing family system reforms.

10.5 Beyond Economics – Non-Economic Dimensions of Societal Development

A society's development is never the result of economic activity alone. Rather, it emerges from the complex interplay of both economic and non-economic factors. While monetary growth, trade, and industry are often emphasized, the deeper fabric of social progress depends equally on elements that are less easily measured but no less influential. For policymakers and economists, understanding these broader forces is essential for designing strategies that foster lasting and inclusive development.

1. **Education and Knowledge**

Education forms the foundation of societal progress. Beyond equipping individuals with the skills necessary for economic participation, it cultivates critical thinking, creativity, and active citizenship. An educated population contributes not only to productivity but also to building an informed and empowered society.

2. **Health and Well-being**

   No society can thrive without a healthy population. Access to healthcare, adequate nutrition, and a clean environment provide the conditions necessary for individuals to flourish. These factors enhance not just physical well-being, but also the productivity and participation required for collective advancement.

3. **Social and Cultural Values**

   Development is deeply shaped by the values, beliefs, and cultural practices that define a society. These influences guide social interactions, determine community priorities, and shape attitudes toward progress. Culture and values create the moral compass by which development is directed.

4. **Political Stability and Governance**

   Effective development relies on governance that is stable, transparent, and participatory. Political stability ensures continuity and order, while accountable institutions safeguard social justice and the rule of law. Together, they provide the environment where economic and social aspirations can take root and grow.

5. **Environmental Sustainability**

Long-term development cannot be separated from the stewardship of natural resources. Sustainable management of land, water, and energy underpins the quality of life of current and future generations. Environmental degradation undermines both economic growth and human well-being, making sustainability a central pillar of true progress.

6. **Social Equity and Inclusion**

   A society that seeks development must also seek fairness. Inclusion of marginalized groups, attention to gender equality, and commitment to social justice ensure that progress benefits all rather than a select few. Equity is not only a moral imperative but also a practical one, as inclusive societies achieve more resilient and sustainable growth.

7. **Community Engagement and Social Capital**

   Trust, cooperation, and community participation significantly enrich development. Social capital—the networks of relationships and shared values that bind individuals—nurtures resilience and collective action. When societies invest in social cohesion, they strengthen their ability to face challenges together.

8. **Peace and Security**

   Conflict and insecurity erode the very foundations of development. Violence hampers economic growth, disrupts institutions, and fractures communities. Conversely, peace provides the conditions in which societies can prosper, innovate, and realize their developmental goals.

9. **Infrastructure and Public Services**

   Basic infrastructure and reliable public services form the backbone of modern life. Transportation networks, electricity, clean water, and sanitation directly improve living standards while enabling economic expansion. Without these fundamental supports, developmental progress remains incomplete.

10. **Technological Advancements**

    Innovation and access to modern technologies act as accelerators of development. Information and communication technologies (ICTs), in particular, expand access to knowledge, enhance productivity, and create new forms of social and economic participation. Technology, when accessible to all, bridges gaps and fosters integration.

Development is neither linear nor one-dimensional. It is a process shaped by economic mechanisms intertwined with non-economic influences that are cultural, political, environmental, and social in nature. Recognizing this reality is crucial for policymakers and economists who aim to design holistic strategies. By embracing the full spectrum of factors–education, health, governance, sustainability, equity, security, community engagement, infrastructure, and technology, societies can move toward sustainable, inclusive, and truly transformative progress.

10.6 Rethinking Development Beyond Monetary Growth

Economists often believe that the complex challenges facing modern societies can be resolved through the expansion of monetary growth. This strategy includes maximizing resource utilization, pooling internal and external resources, increasing money supply, strengthening capital foundations, and fostering technological transformation among other approaches. While such measures can stimulate economic activity, the question remains: *can the true depth of social, political, cultural, and environmental complexity be addressed solely through these methods?*

Throughout history, the world has been graced with noble individuals, visionaries, scientists, ideologists, reformers, educators, and policymakers. Their efforts and recommendations have sought to reform economic societies, guiding them onto the right track and formulating policies for collective betterment. To measure and evaluate progress, several indicators have emerged:

- Social indicators
- Economic indicators
- Political indicators
- Environmental Performance Index

However, the effectiveness of these indicators depends significantly on the positive responsiveness of individuals. Without supportive human behavior and character, even the most comprehensive policy frameworks remain ineffective. This is why some emphasize restructuring the family system as a foundational step, for it influences values, behaviors, and social cohesion factors intrinsically linked with all progress indicators.

10.7 Keynesian Developments and Human Well-being

In recent developments, Neo-Keynesian researchers have increasingly aligned with mainstream economists in focusing on micro-foundations and optimizing behavior. Yet, they continue to highlight themes central to Keynesian thought, such as price and wage inflexibility. Importantly, economics and political science now place greater focus on *well-being* and *quality of life*, moving beyond mere financial metrics to examine factors that directly shape human welfare.

A significant aspect of well-being is the standard of living, often measured by income levels and access to goods and services. These quantifiable metrics, though important, are limited. More intangible dimensions such as freedom, happiness, artistic expression, environmental health, and innovation remain harder to measure. As a result, policy-making often falls into imbalance by prioritizing what is measurable while sidelining aspects that matter deeply to human flourishing.

The Pursuit of Happiness and Indicators of Life Satisfaction

One of the notable steps toward broadening our understanding of well-being came through Adrian White, an analytic social psychologist at the University of Leicester, who developed the *Satisfaction with Life Index*. The field of happiness studies has since grown, intersecting with economics, psychology, and political science. Advances in *positive psychology* have fueled political interest in happiness as a legitimate lens through which to evaluate policy impact.

This gave rise to Happiness Economics, an interdisciplinary field that expands the traditional definition of utility. By including psychological and social well-being alongside traditional economic measures, happiness economics enriches our understanding of national prosperity. Although its effectiveness as a policy-making tool is still evolving, it increasingly complements traditional measures such as GDP and GNP.

Maslow's Hierarchy of Needs

The exploration of human happiness is not new. Abraham Maslow famously theorized that happiness arises from the fulfillment of progressive human needs, arranged in a hierarchical pyramid:

- **Physiological needs:** Basic survival requirements such as food, water, shelter, and rest.
- **Safety needs:** The pursuit of physical security, financial stability, and protection from harm.
- **Love and belonging needs:** The development of social bonds, family connections, friendships, and intimacy.
- **Esteem needs:** The desire for recognition, achievement, accomplishment, and respect.
- **Self-actualization needs:** The highest pursuit is realizing personal potential, creativity, problem-solving, and growth.

Maslow's hierarchy has remained influential for decades. It emphasizes that well-being is layered and multifaceted; individuals climb from immediate survival needs toward higher aspirations of self-realization.

Over time, the concept of happiness has expanded with human society. Once understood primarily in economic terms of wealth and resource possession, it has grown into a far richer and multidimensional pursuit. Today, happiness encompasses:

- Physical health
- Mental and emotional well-being
- Creative expression and innovation
- Deep, meaningful relationships
- A sense of purpose and belonging

The pursuit of happiness is now recognized as a holistic endeavor that reaches beyond income and material wealth. It is about the flourishing of human potential in its physical, psychological, and social dimensions.

The pursuit of development cannot be confined to monetary metrics or economic growth strategies alone. While resource mobilization, technological advancement, and increased capital are important, they are insufficient to resolve the multidimensional challenges of human societies. Indicators, reformist policies, and economic frameworks all have significance, but their true effectiveness relies on human values, collective behavior, and social institutions such as families and communities.

Ultimately, happiness and well-being provide a more profound framework for evaluating progress. By embracing insights from economics, psychology, and sociology alongside Maslow's hierarchy, we move closer to a comprehensive understanding of development. In this vision, true advancement lies not only in wealth creation but in enabling humans to live meaningful, purposeful, and flourishing lives.

In his seminal 1890 work *Principles of Economics*, Alfred Marshall defined economics as "a study of mankind in their everyday economic activities. It explores the aspects of individual and social actions that are most directly related to acquiring and using the material resources necessary for well-being." While Marshall emphasized economic activity as a lens to understand human welfare, the broader canvas of human development reveals that material well-being alone cannot nurture the qualities necessary for building a just and healthy society.

Within the family system, parents often juggle multiple professional and personal responsibilities. This struggle may limit their ability to instill in children essential qualities such as responsibility, accountability, empathy, and social awareness. Many parents, preoccupied with work and business obligations, focus heavily on providing monetary assets and material comforts. While well intended, this approach can foster an illusion of individualism and social superiority rather than nurturing qualities essential for communal well-being.

10.8 The Impact on Children and Society

Children raised in such environments may face emotional neglect, making it difficult for them to develop healthy ways of expressing or managing their emotions. In turn, they may:

- Turn to harmful substances such as drugs
- Engage in inhumane or antisocial activities
- Develop indifference to community needs

- Exhibit violent tendencies and impulsive behavior
- Violate constitutional or ethical boundaries for personal gain.

Such patterns can lead to youth who prioritize pleasure over responsibility, often resorting to destructive behaviors including self-harm and suicide. Others may develop mental disorders, hostility, or social detachment. Ultimately, these struggles hinder their ability to cultivate love, compassion, or meaningful social bonds, leading them into lives marked by loneliness.

Unmet needs play a significant role in this cycle of alienation. According to psychologists, loneliness is not simply being alone, it is a state of disconnection from others, even amid company. Chronic loneliness carries severe social, emotional, and health consequences, including:

- Increased stress levels
- Heightened risk of depression
- Greater likelihood of cardiovascular disease
- Difficulty forming meaningful relationships

This underscores the importance of going beyond meeting only physiological and safety needs. Love, belonging, esteem, and community are equally vital for a well-rounded life. Building authentic relationships, practicing empathy, and creating fulfilling social environments are not luxuries but central necessities for well-being.

In this broader perspective, happiness cannot be understood merely as an individual pursuit. It is, at its core, a collective endeavor. Societies thrive when they build supportive communities that foster inclusivity, compassion, and trust. At the same time, families serve as the first school of socialization. Without this foundation, children remain unable to distinguish true happiness from fleeting satisfaction, often living under illusions of success or pleasure.

The consequences extend beyond individual struggles, reflecting at a macroeconomic level. Antisocial behavior and social unrest harm national productivity, eroding GDP and undermining collective prosperity. Even current methods of measuring GDP risk overemphasizing monetary activity while ignoring the deeper well-being of populations therefore perpetuating illusionary notions of growth and development.

Restructuring Family Priorities

To reverse these trends, restructuring family priorities is necessary. Parents, especially mothers, who play a central nurturing role must dedicate intentional effort toward raising children with compassion, care, and awareness. Until this shift occurs, the aforementioned societal issues are bound to persist and potentially intensify in the future.

A mother's involvement becomes critical when she embraces her role with reverence and devotion, showering children with love while also instilling values of empathy, accountability, and responsibility.

- How to manage their emotions, even in challenging circumstances

- How to interact respectfully with peers and colleagues

- How to balance personal rights with responsibility toward

society

- How to cultivate patriotism and social consciousness
- How to respect elders, traditions, and societal frameworks

When this foundation is in place, children grow not only into capable individuals but also into socially responsible citizens who strengthen the moral and cultural fabric of society.

Marshall's insight that economics studies human activity in everyday life still holds true today but reducing human well-being to material resources alone overlooks the deeper truths of social progress. Families remain at the heart of development, shaping not just individual character but societal future. When parents, especially mothers, commit fully to nurturing emotional strength, communal awareness, and human dignity, they create children capable of true happiness not illusionary satisfaction and societies capable of harmony, stability, and sustainable progress.

Teaching individuals how to interact with others, manage their emotions, and cultivate social values such as patriotism, respect, and responsibility are essential elements of healthy social and emotional development. These capabilities are not innate but must be intentionally taught, modeled, and practiced across different stages of life.

1. **Emotional Regulation**

   Emotional regulation is the foundation of self-control and maturity. It refers to the ability to understand, manage, and respond to emotions in a balanced manner. To cultivate this ability, individuals can practice mindfulness, deep breathing, and self-reflection. Children and adults alike should be encouraged to recognize and label their emotions, identify triggers, and employ healthy coping strategies to manage stress or conflict.

2. **Social Interaction Skills**

   Effective social interaction skills are critical for building relationships and fostering cooperation. These can be developed by teaching active listening, empathy, respect for boundaries, and effective communication. Non-verbal language, such as eye contact and body posture, should also be emphasized, as they shape how individuals connect with others.

3. **Positive Peer Interactions**

   Relationships with peers and colleagues play a crucial role in identity formation and social trust. Encouraging respect, kindness, and teamwork creates stronger social bonds. Teaching conflict-resolution strategies, compromise, and negotiation helps individuals contribute constructively to society. Participation in group activities that foster collaboration instills a stronger sense of belonging and community.

4. **Patriotism and Civic Responsibility**

   Patriotism, when combined with civic responsibility, nurtures an understanding that individual success is intimately tied to collective prosperity. This requires educating individuals about their country's history, values, and democratic principles. Participation in civic duties such as voting, volunteering, and engaging in community service reaffirms the importance of justice, equality, and accountability in society.

5. **Understanding Rights and Responsibilities**

   For a society to flourish, individuals must understand both their rights and their responsibilities. Valuing diversity and protecting the rights of others allows communities to thrive. By cultivating active citizenship, societies develop a stronger sense of unity, fairness, and shared obligation.

6. **Respect for Elders**

   Respecting elders is a value that binds families and strengthens cultural continuity. Encouraging children to listen to the wisdom of their elders, appreciate their contributions, and learn from their experiences fosters humility and gratitude. Inter-generational gatherings and community activities provide opportunities for such learning.

Strong moral values enhance trust, promote peace, and encourage responsible behavior. These intangible qualities; loyalty, discernment, authenticity, joy, peace of mind, and trustworthiness contribute immensely to social stability and productivity. If cultivated at scale, such values could contribute the equivalent of 70–80 percent to a nation's GDP by ensuring smoother governance, higher social efficiency, and reduced conflict. The transformation of individuals into morally conscious citizens would enable societies to address challenges swiftly and achieve development goals more easily.

10.9 The Mother's Role in Emotional and Social Formation

Across human history, mothers have played a uniquely intimate role in shaping children's emotional behavior, values, and character. A mother's bond enables her to notice even the slightest changes in her children, guiding them through adolescence, shifting attitudes, and generational differences. Her nurturing role often grants her a natural sensitivity to both positive and negative emotional states, empowering her to provide guidance, comfort, and correction.

Yet, while mothers play this profound role, other caregivers: fathers, grandparents, teachers, and community members also contribute meaningfully to children's development. A child raised within a broad and healthy support network benefits not only from maternal intuition, but also from diverse perspectives and models of behavior. Open communication and active listening across this network create a safe environment where children can express themselves freely.

Still, the unparalleled role of mothers must not be overlooked. In many ways, societies fail to recognize and honor the essential services mothers provide, even while investing heavily in education systems, technology, and infrastructure. Ironically, while the world has institutions dedicated to raising pets with exceptional care, it lacks equivalent institutions devoted to raising children holistically. In practice, this responsibility falls most profoundly upon mothers who embody a divine capacity for nurturing growth and well-being.

Neglecting the Power of Nurturing

As societies preoccupy themselves with material accomplishments and trivial occupations, they risk squandering the profound generational power mothers hold. Overlooking the nurturing capacity of women, particularly mothers, creates cracks at every level: individual, familial, societal, and national. Our current and future challenges economic, cultural, and moral alike remain deeply tied to this fundamental oversight.

Emotional regulation, social interaction skills, civic responsibility, respect for others, and moral values lay the foundation of both personal fulfillment and collective prosperity. While these skills can be taught and modeled across communities, the primary and most profound site of their nurturing remains the family and at its heart, the mother. In recognizing the mother's unparalleled role, while also valuing the contributions of other caregivers, society can achieve a balance that supports both individual flourishing and national development.

The future well-being of nations may depend less on economic strategies alone and more on how deeply we honor and support the essential work of mothers who quietly shape the values and emotional lives of every coming generation.

Women are often wiser than men and equally capable if not more of performing any given task with dedication and efficiency. Yet, there exist certain roles that only mothers can fulfill, roles so unique that no substitutes can replace them in the universe. While fathers may contribute meaningfully to a child's upbringing, their efforts alone are often insufficient or less optimal in comparison to the deep nurturing bond that mothers provide. In this sense, women, through their maternal roles, can drive societal progress for one generation, yet it is essential to consider how future generations bear the long-term effects of the family structures and values established today.

Parenting is not a one-sided responsibility. Each parent brings unique strengths, perspectives, and approaches to raising children. Mothers often have a special, intimate connection with their children, especially in early developmental stages. At the same time, fathers make equally valuable contributions, serving as strong role models, offering emotional support, and shaping children's growth and identity.

While some roles are more commonly associated with mothers due to biological and social reasons, this does not diminish the potential contributions of fathers. In fact, an inclusive and balanced approach to parenting where both mothers and fathers actively engage; Creates optimal conditions for producing well-rounded and socially responsible children.

It is therefore essential not to reinforce confining stereotypes or rigid gender roles that restrict the capacity of either men or women. Both have unique contributions, and together they enrich not only the family unit but society at large.

Societal growth should not be attributed to one gender alone. Progress is a collective effort that requires the collaboration of men and women alike across all areas of life–parenting, education, work, leadership, and community participation. By recognizing and valuing different strengths, skills, and perspectives from both genders, societies ensure inclusivity, strengthen resilience, and promote sustainability for future generations.

10.10 Dysfunctional Families and Their Broader Consequences

When families fail in their nurturing role, the consequences extend far beyond the children themselves. Dysfunctional family environments can produce ripple effects throughout society, resulting in:

- Emotional instability and poor mental health
- Behavioral issues and impaired social development
- Weak interpersonal relationships and lack of empathy
- Increased risks of substance abuse, crime, and violence
- Reduced opportunities for education and employment

The result is a cycle of disadvantage that not only impacts individuals but also hinders governments, economists, and social institutions from extending meaningful benefits to vulnerable populations. Governments, in particular, find it more difficult to administer social justice, ensure equity, and uphold peace and harmony when large segments of the population grow disconnected from familial support structures.

Individuals emerging from dysfunctional family systems often lack the support, resources, and values needed to thrive. Consequently, they enter adulthood unprepared to form stable relationships, access economic opportunities, or contribute positively to civic life. These gaps intensify social and economic inequality and perpetuate cycles of poverty.

Governments are then tasked with responding to heightened pressures addressing rising crime rates, providing welfare assistance, and bridging gaps in education and healthcare. Thus, the quality of family environments directly influences political stability, social equity, and long-term economic growth.

The family is the cornerstone of individual development and collective progress. While maternal roles are irreplaceable, and fathers play equally critical parts, it is their combined and complementary contributions that give children the resilience, empathy, and moral foundation to thrive. To ignore the importance of nurturing families is to overlook the root cause of many societal challenges from crime and inequality to weakened governance and economic stagnation.

The future of nations, therefore, depends not only on economic systems or technological advancements but also on the strength, stability, and inclusivity of family structures. By valuing and reinforcing both maternal and paternal contributions, while addressing dysfunction within families, societies can nurture future generations capable of ensuring justice, peace, and sustainable progress.

The impacts of dysfunctional family environments are profound, extending far beyond individual households to shape broader social and economic outcomes. Addressing these impacts requires a multi-pronged approach, involving not just families but also communities, policymakers, and institutions.

Pathways to Address Dysfunctional Family Systems:

1. **Social Support Services**

   Expanding access to counseling, therapy, and family support programs can help individuals and families confront psycho-social challenges. Such services promote healthy communication, rebuild trust, and instill coping strategies essential for stable relationships.

2. **Education**

   Parenting education, conflict resolution skills, and training in emotional regulation are crucial tools in building stronger families. By equipping parents and couples with the ability to navigate crises constructively, education becomes a preventive measure against dysfunction.

3. **Community Engagement**

   Communities act as critical support networks that reduce isolation. Encouraging community connections through programs, social activities, and volunteerism helps families find resilience in collective solidarity.

4. **Economic Support**

   Financial pressures are often at the root of family

breakdown. Targeted interventions that alleviate poverty, provide employment opportunities, and strengthen household incomes can alleviate the stressors that lead to dysfunction.

5. **Legal and Policy Measures**

   Strong legal protections that uphold the rights of children and other vulnerable family members safeguard against abuse, exploitation, and neglect. Family-friendly policies embedded within governance structures set a framework for long-term stability.

This multi-sectoral approach recognizes that dysfunctional family environments are complex and multifaceted issues. They can only be effectively addressed through collaborative efforts between individuals, families, communities, and governments.

Most economic policies from classical to modern schools of thought, share objectives of ensuring happy, prosperous, and equitable societies. Yet, these goals often remain elusive. The reason is not just inadequacy in economic models, but the deeper challenge of human behavior and values. Individuals are frequently guided by self-interest, wealth accumulation, and corrupt intentions, undermining the moral and ethical foundations upon which sound policy depends. Emotions like greed, envy, fear play a greater role than policymakers acknowledge. As a result, even sophisticated policies may falter in execution.

The solution lies not solely in crafting better economic strategies, but in reforming the family system as the starting point of societal behavior. Families serve as the primary sites of value transmission and moral development. Healthy family environments instill empathy, cooperation, respect, and accountability; qualities that transform policy objectives into lived realities.

Several measures can strengthen family institutions and promote social stability and national development:

- **Promote healthy relationships** through education on communication, partnerships, and conflict resolution.
- **Encourage positive parenting** by equipping parents with strategies fostering emotional and psychological well-being in children.
- **Provide support to families in need** through social services, subsidies, and community programs mitigating stresses like poverty, illness, or breakdown.
- **Create family-friendly policies** including parental leave, flexible work arrangements, and affordable childcare.
- **Foster community engagement** to build strong social networks reinforcing family values and inter-generational support.

These measures affirm families as interconnected pillars of communities and economies. Reforming the family system builds a foundation for ethical, compassionate, and resilient societies.

10.11 Case Studies of Family Reform and Impact

Nordic Countries: Progressive Family-Friendly Policies

Nordic nations such as Sweden, Denmark, Norway, Finland, and Iceland are global examples of family-friendly policy frameworks. For instance, Sweden offers parents 480 days of parental leave per child, with specific non-transferable portions reserved for fathers to promote equitable caregiving. Denmark caps childcare fees and prioritizes outdoor education, while Norway ensures paid leave with incentives for paternal involvement. These policies have led to increased gender equality, stronger parent-child bonds, improved child development outcomes, higher workforce participation (especially of women), and better overall societal well-being.

Asia: Household Systems and Economic Growth

Asia's rapid economic growth is closely intertwined with evolving family structures. The rise of Asia's middle class has fueled domestic demand, driving sustainable economic growth and decreased vulnerability to external shocks. Household consumption, improved education, and healthcare mirror rising incomes. These changes foster long-term productivity and stronger social institutions. Moreover, family-based networks in many Asian cultures provide informal social safety nets that mitigate risks and support entrepreneurship and economic stability. Yet disparities remain in rural vs urban access and gender equality, creating areas to strengthen through policy and cultural shifts.

Africa: Extended Family and Community-Based Models

African communities traditionally operate with extended family and communal caregiving systems. Unlike Western nuclear family models, African families involve kin networks responsible for widows, orphans, and vulnerable members, ensuring social security through shared obligations. A man's failure to support widowed relatives invites social sanction, reinforcing community cohesion and stability. Such collectivist models emphasize social justice, pluralism, and interconnectedness. However, modernization and Western influences strain these traditions, challenging continuity. Community-driven social innovations continue to support families through literacy

References

Aghion, P., & Howitt, P. (1992). *A model of growth through creative destruction. Econometrica, 60*(2), 323–351.

Admati, A. R., & Hellwig, M. F. (2013). *The bankers' new clothes: What's wrong with banking and what to do about it*. Princeton University Press.

Acemoglu, D., & Robinson, J. A. (2012). *Why nations fail: The origins of power, prosperity, and poverty*. Crown.

Atkinson, A. B. (2015). *Inequality: What can be done?* Harvard University Press.

Beck, U. (1992). *Risk society: Toward a new modernity*. Sage Publications.

Chang, H. (2002). *Kicking away the ladder: Development strategy in historical perspective*. Anthem Press.

Coase, R. H. (1960). The problem of social cost. *Journal of Law and Economics, 3*, 1–44.

Collier, P. (2007). *The bottom billion: Why the poorest countries are failing and what can be done about it*. Oxford University Press.

Daly, H. E. (1992). *Steady-state economics* (2nd ed.). Island Press.

Daly, H. E. (1996). *Beyond growth: The economics of sustainable development*. Beacon Press.

Dasgupta, P. (2009). The concept of social capital and its application to the economics of rural investment. *Oxford Economic Papers, 61*(2), 113–149.

Dasgupta, P. (2021). *The economics of biodiversity: The Dasgupta review.* HM Treasury.

Easterly, W. (2001). *The elusive quest for growth: Economists' adventures and misadventures in the tropics.* MIT Press.

Easterly, W. (2006). *The white man's burden.* Penguin.

Friedman, M. (1962). *Capitalism and freedom.* University of Chicago Press.

Hausmann, R., Hwang, J., & Rodrik, D. (2007). What you export matters. *Journal of Economic Growth, 12*(1), 1–25.

Hausmann, R., & Hidalgo, C. A. (2014). *The atlas of economic complexity: Mapping paths to prosperity.* MIT Press.

Hidalgo, C. A., & Hausmann, R. (2009). The building blocks of economic complexity. *PNAS, 106*(26), 10570–10575.

Hirschman, A. O. (1958). *The strategy of economic development.* Yale University Press.

Hotelling, H. (1931). The economics of exhaustible resources. *Journal of Political Economy, 39*(2), 137–175.

Howlett, M., & Ramesh, M. (2003). *Studying public policy: Policy cycles and policy subsystems* (2nd ed.). Oxford University Press.

IPCC. (2023). *Climate change 2023: Synthesis report.* Cambridge University Press.

Kahneman, D. (2011). *Thinking, fast and slow.* Farrar, Straus and Giroux.

Keynes, J. M. (1936). *The general theory of employment, interest and money.* Macmillan.

Kingdon, J. W. (1984). *Agendas, alternatives, and public policies.* Little, Brown.

Kirman, A. (1992). Whom or what does the representative individual represent? *Journal of Economic Perspectives, 6*(2), 117–136.

Kremer, M. (1993). The O-ring theory of economic development. *Quarterly Journal of Economics, 108*(3), 551–575.

Krugman, P. (1991). *Geography and trade*. MIT Press.

Kuznets, S. (1955). Economic growth and income inequality. *American Economic Review, 45*(1), 1–28.

Lewis, W. A. (1954). Economic development with unlimited supplies of labor. *Manchester School, 22*, 139–191.

Lindblom, C. E. (1959). The science of "muddling through." *Public Administration Review, 19*(2), 79–88.

Lucas, R. E. (1976). Econometric policy evaluation: A critique. *Carnegie–Rochester Conference Series on Public Policy, 1*, 19–46.

Lucas, R. E. (1988). On the mechanics of economic development. *Journal of Monetary Economics, 22*(1), 3–42.

Marshall, A. (1890). *Principles of economics*. Macmillan.

Marx, K. (1867). *Capital: A critique of political economy* (Vol. 1). Hamburg.

Mazzucato, M. (2013). *The entrepreneurial state*. Anthem Press.

Mazzucato, M. (2018). *The value of everything: Making and taking in the global economy*. Allen Lane.

Meadows, D. H., Meadows, D. L., Randers, J., & Behrens, W. W. (1972). *The limits to growth*. Universe Books.

Minsky, H. P. (1986). *Stabilizing an unstable economy*. Yale University Press.

Myrdal, G. (1968). *Asian drama: An inquiry into the poverty of nations*. Pantheon.

North, D. C. (1990). *Institutions, institutional change and economic performance*. Cambridge University Press.

Nurkse, R. (1953). *Problems of capital formation in underdeveloped coun-*

tries. Oxford University Press.

Ostrom, E. (1990). *Governing the commons*. Cambridge University Press.

Piketty, T. (2014). *Capital in the twenty-first century*. Harvard University Press.

Pigou, A. C. (1920). *The economics of welfare*. Macmillan.

Polanyi, K. (1944). *The great transformation*. Rinehart.

Putnam, R. D. (1993). *Making democracy work: Civic traditions in modern Italy*. Princeton University Press.

Putnam, R. D. (2000). *Bowling alone: The collapse and revival of American community*. Simon & Schuster.

Rawls, J. (1971). *A theory of justice*. Harvard University Press.

Ricardo, D. (1817). *On the principles of political economy and taxation*. John Murray.

Rockström, J., Steffen, W., Noone, K., Persson, Å., Chapin, F. S., III, … Foley, J. A. (2009). Planetary boundaries: Exploring the safe operating space for humanity. *Ecology and Society, 14*(2), 32.

Rodrik, D. (2004). *Industrial policy for the twenty-first century*. UNIDO.

Rodrik, D. (2007). *One economics, many recipes*. Princeton University Press.

Romer, P. M. (1986). Increasing returns and long-run growth. *Journal of Political Economy, 94*(5), 1002–1037.

Rostow, W. W. (1960). *The stages of economic growth: A non-communist manifesto*. Cambridge University Press.

Sabatier, P. A., & Jenkins-Smith, H. C. (1993). *Policy change and learning*. Westview Press.

Sachs, J. D. (2005). *The end of poverty*. Penguin.

Sachs, J. D. (2015). *The age of sustainable development*. Columbia University Press.

Schumpeter, J. A. (1942). *Capitalism, socialism and democracy*. Harper & Brothers.

Seers, D. (1969). The meaning of development. *International Development Review, 11*(4), 3–14.

Sen, A. (1981). *Poverty and famines*. Oxford University Press.

Sen, A. (1985). *Commodities and capabilities*. North-Holland.

Sen, A. (1999). *Development as freedom*. Oxford University Press.

Smith, A. (1776). *The wealth of nations*. W. Strahan and T. Cadell.

Solow, R. M. (1956). A contribution to the theory of economic growth. *Quarterly Journal of Economics, 70*(1), 65–94.

Stiglitz, J. E. (1989). Markets, market failures, and development. *American Economic Review, 79*(2), 197–203.

Stiglitz, J. E. (2010). *Freefall*. W. W. Norton.

Stiglitz, J. E. (2012). *The price of inequality*. W. W. Norton.

Stiglitz, J. E., Sen, A., & Fitoussi, J.-P. (2010). *Mismeasuring our lives*. The New Press.

Streeten, P. (1981). *First things first*. Oxford University Press.

Sutton, J., & Trefler, D. (2016). Capabilities, wealth, and trade. *Journal of Political Economy, 124*(3), 826–878.

Tietenberg, T., & Lewis, L. (2018). *Environmental and natural resource economics* (11th ed.). Routledge.

Thaler, R. H., & Sunstein, C. R. (2008). *Nudge*. Yale University Press.

Todaro, M. P., & Smith, S. C. (2015). *Economic development* (12th ed.). Pearson.

United Nations. (1987). *Our common future*. Oxford University Press.

United Nations. (2015). *Transforming our world: The 2030 agenda for sustainable development*. United Nations.

United Nations Development Programme. (1990). *Human development report 1990*. Oxford University Press.

United Nations Development Programme. (2019). *Human development report 2019*. UNDP.

Wilkinson, R. G., & Pickett, K. (2009). *The spirit level*. Allen Lane.

World Bank. (1991). *World development report 1991*. Oxford University Press.

World Bank. (2005). *World development report 2005: Equity and development*. World Bank.

World Bank. (2012). *Inclusive green growth*. World Bank.

World Bank. (2020). *Poverty and shared prosperity 2020*. World Bank.

World Economic Forum. (2023). *The global risks report 2023*. World Economic Forum.

www.ingramcontent.com/pod-product-compliance
Ingram Content Group UK Ltd.
Pitfield, Milton Keynes, MK11 3LW, UK
UKHW021402190726
13845UKWH00028B/833

9 789373 158822